LA⎯⎯⎯⎯

THE AUTOBIOGRAPHY

by

Roderick Wood

Grosvenor House
Publishing Limited

This book is published by
Grosvenor House Publishing Ltd
28-30 High Street, Guildford, Surrey, GU1 3EL.
www.grosvenorhousepublishing.co.uk

A CIP record for this book
is available from the British Library

ISBN 978-1-78148-907-9

This book is dedicated to my mum.

Contents

Introduction

On February 12th 2014 I died.

My heart stopped for 27 minutes.

Medically speaking, I was dead.

Without the professional skill of the life guards – and two other staff members at the David Lloyd gym – I'd now be on the other side. Without hesitating, they put their first aid skills into use, breathing life into a person who was very nearly gone for good. I can't thank them enough for their quick thinking and bravery in such a terrible and stressful situation.

They say there's no coming back from a thing like that, and I guess I'm the exception to the rule. It's been tough – harder than I would ever have imagined – but I'm finally getting my life back on track.

So, how did it happen? It started out pretty regular, just a normal day like any other, with me going to my local gym to work out. Keeping fit and healthy is important to me, but I had no idea when I walked through those doors that morning that I almost wouldn't make it back out again.

It was a regular session: an hour of rowing, running and cross-training. I liked the feeling of exercise, of knowing that I was helping my body be the best it could be so I could be the best *I* could be. At 52 years old, you really have to start thinking about these things, and I thought about it perhaps a little more often than most.

I think this is why it came as such a big shock – I was healthy, wasn't I? So why did this happen to me?

I'd just finished my session and, as usual, decided to round it off with a trip to the sauna area. I changed into my trunks, walked over to the Jacuzzi, and that's when it happened. My heart stopped. It stopped dead.

People ask me: What was it like? Was there a light at the end of the tunnel? What did I see? Could I view myself from above? Was I aware of what was happening?

They want all these answers, whether they're spiritual or religious or not. It's just human nature, isn't it? We all want to know what happens to us when we die, when we pass over to the other side. Is there a Heaven? A Hell? Does what we do in life impact how we are in death? What about reincarnation? Is there even anything at all?

These questions, of course, have plagued humanity since the beginning of time, and I'm afraid I can't answer them specifically, but when I dream sometimes, I do remember things I can't explain. Impressions of total peace and total calm surround me at these times, and that feeling is comforting in a way I can't fully express. When I dream of these emotions, it feels as though I'm ready for my next life, for the next phase, whatever that may be. I feel satisfied with what I've achieved and prepared for the future.

However, it wasn't meant to be – I was meant to come back and live my life out here, as I always assumed I would (after all, no one likes to think about when or how they're going to die, and I was no different). I'm now looking forward to the next thirty years of my life, and everything I can achieve within those years. It'll be a little harder, now, after the past few months I've had, but I'm glad I'm here to live them.

Immediately after the heart attack, I don't really remember much. In fact, I don't remember much for the first four weeks or so of my hospital stay. Of course, I've since found out that my ex-wife and eldest son were taken into a cold, clinical room by the doctor and told that I had suffered from severe brain damage as a result of the heart attack. They were told that I'd be like a goldfish in a bowl, alive but limited – very limited. It hurts to think of them having to go through this, but it feels good that I proved the doctors wrong.

Eight months have passed since that fateful day at the gym, and with all the tremendous positive energy and prayers sent to me by friends and family, I'm nearly recovered. I'm not like a goldfish in a bowl. My brain is still a bit slow, I admit, but it wasn't that quick before...

It sometimes takes an incident like this – as horrific and painful as it was – to put things into perspective. Having a heart attack really makes you think, about your life as it is now, and how you've lived it for all these years. Did I make the right decisions? Did I do what I wanted to do? Did I put things off? Was I really as happy as I could have been?

People generally start asking themselves these questions when they get to around seventy or eighty years old, but I can tell you now, people who've lived through heart attacks ask them too. The whole experience really made me take stock of my life and the things I'd done in the past. If I had died that day at the gym, my children wouldn't even know half of what I'd done in my life, wouldn't know the kind of person I was when I was young, and wouldn't know what I truly felt about all kinds of things. This is a deeply worrying thought.

If you were to die today, suddenly, with no preparation and nothing in place in the event of such a terrible tragedy, would your family and friends know all about your past? The experiences you're proud of and the ones you aren't? If you were to die, so would thousands of memories and years of knowledge, hundreds of experiences and feelings and emotions.

This is why I decided to get my life story down on paper, where it will stay, should anyone in my family or any of my friends decide they want to know about me, the real me, either while I'm still here or once I'm gone.

Sometimes, it takes a heart attack to make you think.

I've gone through a lot, but I've never given up.

I want this book to show you who I am.

I also want it to be a testament to the fact that no matter what life throws at you, you can get through it and come out the other end smiling.

I did it, and so can you.

Chapter One

So, French kissing my girlfriend's grandmother at her 80th birthday party probably wasn't the smartest thing to do. In my defence, I wasn't really myself that night – I was high on dope and speed, and a lot of booze to boot, but that's no excuse.

I guess you could say I used to have a bit of a hedonistic lifestyle. Like many young people, I absolutely lived for the weekends; when 5 p.m. on Friday rolled around, I was the happiest guy there was. Honestly, if someone were to put me in a coma from Monday morning until Friday afternoon, I'd have been perfectly content.

I supposed I'd better go right back to the day I was born. The date was 10th of March 1962, it was at Worthing Hospital, and I was the youngest of three boys. An ordinary birth, nothing too special, but my parents were perhaps not quite so usual; my mother was a beautiful Austrian woman who had come over and married my father, a classic brutish Englishman.

I suppose my mother was typical of women in her generation, staying at home in our council house and making sure everything was perfect for her husband. She was subservient and quiet, with her main aim every day to have the tea on the table whenever my father got in from work. This wasn't quite the easy task it could have been, as the time varied quite often depending on how long my father spent at the pub afterwards. He was a heavy drinker, and he'd often have a few down at the local before coming home to his family and his food.

If he came back after 8 p.m., we knew it was going to be a stormy night; he'd bang through the back gate and march in through the door, not even trying to keep the noise down. This was a sign that he was pissed, and it was a sign me and my brothers knew all too well.

My mum would warm his dinner for him – after it had inevitably gone cold while we waited for him to come home – and then the three of us would scatter, not wanting to be around him for the next part of the evening.

We'd hear it, though. At first, it would be quiet, and I've never known – before or since – a silence to be so noisy! We'd wait for it to begin, and begin it always would. It started with our father shouting at my mother about the quality of the food. Of course, he didn't put it quite like that:

"What is this shit? I've been out working hard all day and I have to come home to this? Why did you even dish this shite up to me?"

It was his customary call and the signal for another sleepless night, for all of us.

My father wasn't a very nice man. He would rant and rave and swear and moan – generally, he was just truly nasty. Often – to me, anyway – he seemed like a madman; it was quite frightening. When he was like this, I'd leave the house, happy to just wander the streets for a while until the early hours. I'd only come back when I was sure he'd be asleep in his chair and therefore unable to say or do anything to me.

Strangely, the day after one of these occurrences, it would never be mentioned at all – nothing would be said about the previous night, or about his disgusting behaviour towards his wife and his children. It was as if by not allowing us to speak of it, my father could pretend like it had never happened. But it did, far too many times.

Not to give him an excuse for his behaviour, but he had been in the North Sea Convoys during World War Two, and I suppose that took its toll – both on him and us.

I grew up in a rough neighbourhood in Worthing. Our council house was on an estate that had a pretty bad reputation, and I tried to keep my address a secret from my school friends because of this; if I was invited to any parties, for instance, I wouldn't let them know where I lived.

It wasn't just me, either. My brother loved tennis and wanted to join the West Worthing tennis club, but when they found out his address, they 'politely declined'. It was ridiculous.

The actual estate was a bit of a mess. There were a lot of trainers flung over telephone cables, graffiti, the odd car with no wheels, propped up by bricks, that kind of thing. Most of the actual houses, though in a bad condition, were well kept and clean, so that was something, I suppose.

My own house had three bedrooms, a bathroom, a toilet, a front room, a dining room and a kitchen. It had a small back garden, an asbestos roof, and concrete skirting and door frames. The only heating we had came from an open fire in the front room and a wood boiler in the kitchen. It was pretty basic.

Winters were the worst. One year, I remember it being so cold that I wrote my name on the frost on the windows – from inside the house. It was so freezing that getting out of bed in the morning was a massive chore, and I would only slip out from under the covers once I'd heard the wood being chopped to fire up the boiler. The kindling usually consisted of beer crates, old chair legs, pallets... that sort of thing. Basically, anything my mum could find. I remember that on cold, wintry mornings, I'd have to huddle around the boiler to get warm before I could even consider getting changed into my school clothes.

Sometimes we'd have to push my dad's van to help it start, something that was no fun whatsoever in the freezing temperatures. This was the late 60s and it was a little Bedford van with a wind-up handle – how things have advanced! In the late 60s and early 70s we really struggled to keep warm; there were no radiators, no continental quilts, and no double glazing – not on the Maybridge estate, anyway.

Because of this, I remember that every year, the winters seemed to start earlier and earlier, forcing us to battle through more days of freezing cold each time the season rolled around. One year, it seemed that it was much colder on Bonfire Night than any other time.

Bonfire Night was legendary – if that's the right word – where we lived. On November 5th, my brothers would dress me up as a Guy in a mask and sit me outside the local sweetshop where I'd ask, "Penny for the Guy?"

When it came to actual fireworks displays, however, the estate always resembled Beirut. As fireworks were so easy to get hold of, there would be a two week war around November 5th, which was both loud and incredibly dangerous. We'd have to put up with days and days of bangers, air bombs, jumping jacks, air bomb repeaters and many more. Bangers were like little sticks of dynamite and air bombs... well, they were just unbelievable.

It really was like a mini war. Air bombs were let off inside flat entrances and houses belonging to old people, rockets were set off, strategically aimed at different gangs in the area, and bangers were lit and put inside milk bottles, which when thrown, caused glass-shattering explosions. It was a frightening time for some people on the estate, no matter how old they were.

Every year, a huge bonfire would be made, and pretty much anything was used to build it up – whatever people could get their hands on, whether it belonged to them or not.

One year, a local lad made a homemade bomb of one hundred bangers taped together. This boy just so happened to be a school bully, and he would often take my school dinner money off me at knifepoint. He thought he was clever making this homemade bomb, but unfortunately for him, it blew up in his dad's shed. Obviously, this was karma working on my behalf; he was badly burned and had to stay off school for a while, leaving my lunch money – and that of others – temporarily safe. What goes around comes around.

By the time I got to 11 years old, I was the skinny, athletic type. I was good at most sports I tried my hand at, but I particularly loved football – both watching and playing.

Just as I passed the 11 plus exam, it was scrapped, and at the age of twelve the government made me go to the nearest school according to my religion. This was the Chatsmore Catholic High School, which was full of students of various ethnicities, including a lot of Italians.

It wasn't as good as the school both my brothers attended (The Worthing High School) and I wished I'd been able to go there instead. Incidentally, my brother Robert ended up with a degree from Oxford, and my brother Richard gained two degrees from the Imperial College London.

I had quite a few friends when I was young but one of them really stood out for me. His name was Mark and he was a neighbour. The same age as me, we'd grown up together since we were just one year old. We were typical boys and we had some great times as young kids – we were always into mischief.

One time, Mark put a rope going from his toilet window across to mine, and the plan was for us to walk along the rope and get into each other's houses. I tried first, and it didn't go too well – I took one step on the rope and then dropped like a stone, landing on my arse. Due to the soft landing, it didn't hurt too much.

Another time, however, led to quite a bit more pain. Mark and I had made a camp in a nearby field out of all sorts of rubbish, using a tarpaulin for a roof. It was a great little den, and our friend Karen (around eleven years old at the time) came inside to have a look. Well, Mark and I took advantage of the situation and told her that she couldn't leave until she'd dropped her knickers. We were young and we wanted to have a look at a fanny for the first time – at that point, the only ones we'd seen belonged to our mothers, not something you wanted to think about too much. Anyway, she was actually pretty happy to do this, which was great for us – until she told her sister, that is. Her sister then told her mum, and all these years later, I can still feel the pain of those smacks we got as punishment!

I wasn't into the academic side of school too much but I had skills in other areas. For instance, I still loved football and I actually became captain of the school team, staying in that position until I left. By the age of thirteen, I could swear in five different languages and I knew how to finger a girl – not the kind of thing they teach in school.

To play football, my dad thought that my brother's old rugby boots would be adequate. They weren't. Then, however, I joined Manor Athletic. This was a youth team (in the Worthing youth league) that my friend and next door neighbour also joined, and when I started playing for them, the manager bought me a pair of new Adidas mitres – beautiful!

It was at Manor Athletic that I met Steve Hart, who was the goalkeeper. He'd recently moved down from South London and I suppose, in a way, Steve took over from Mark; as we'd gone to different schools, we'd drifted apart over the years, especially when I really got into football (Mark wasn't that good at football, or at all interested in it really).

I played as much as possible, and we were lucky in that a bit of land behind the crescent was great for using as a pitch – it was behind the back gardens of the houses, which formed a perfect stadium. From about the age of ten, I'd go to that 'pitch', where about twenty other local kids used to meet, and we'd always find someone to have a knockabout with, or even have a full-on match by ourselves. I was always there, come rain or shine. I just loved it.

So, because of our interest in football, Steve and I became good buddies. Apart from the love of the game, however, he was sort of the opposite of me in many ways. For one thing, he lived in a big house in East Worthing (with his parents and his brother), right on the seafront. It was great and I have brilliant memories from those days. Steve loved horses, and he'd used to talk all the time about how he wanted to be a Canadian Mountie. This got passed onto me a little bit, and one summer my dad even paid for me to go with Steve on a week's holiday to The Flying G Ranch in the New Forest. This probably wouldn't have happened if my dad and Steve's dad hadn't become drinking buddies, and I think he was reluctant to fork out the money, but I was happy to go no matter what the circumstances.

It was such a fantastic time. Apart from one night in Bridport with Mum and Dad, I'd never been on holiday before, so just the thought of it kept me excited for weeks. Steve and I each had a horse, which we were responsible for during our stay – this meant looking after it, grooming it, and riding it, which we did every day. We'd go out for two hours in the morning and two in the afternoon, accompanied by a cowboy from Southampton. There was ranch style food, which meant plenty of beans, and plenty of farting, like the Blazing Saddles film. I took to horse riding surprisingly well and rarely fell off, but by the end of the week, my arse was incredibly sore!

We were always doing fun stuff as teenagers, and the football continued to go really well; I played for some Sussex schools and we got quite far in the national trophy.

Although girls were more Steve's thing than mine, I'd had my fair share of early teenage experiences. These came in the form of a couple of hand jobs and some heavy petting, up until I was about fifteen. By then, I was the only virgin among our group and so Steve organised for 'the local bike' to accommodate me. Her name was Paula and she was a Vicar's daughter. Seventeen years old, she was quite plump and had constantly greasy hair – not very attractive. Still, she was willing, and one day when Steve's house was empty, I went round to lose my virginity.

Me, Steve, Nige and Chris sat in the front room and chatted to Paula, who had a glass of wine and then took Nige into Steve's bedroom. I waited nervously outside until Nige came out, grinning at me. I heard her shout, "Wheel him in!" and when I went in, she was lying on the bed, naked.

"Get your kit off then," she said, getting straight to the point. Still nervous, I undressed quickly and lay next to her, my cock hard and ready. She looked at it before giving me instructions: "I'll suck it a bit then you can slide it in, OK?" I nodded, not knowing what to say, and she started sucking. Only a few seconds had gone by, but as I was almost ready to shoot, I stopped her.

"Quick!" I shouted, as I rolled on top of her and let her guide me in. As soon as I'd entered her, she wrapped her legs around me, and after one thrust, I shot. It was over.

"That it?" she asked. "Fuck me. Oh well, get the other one in – I need a fuck."

I went out with the biggest grin on my face – I wasn't a virgin anymore!

With that, Paula finished with the other two, hopped on her moped, and sped off.

* * *

School was OK, I suppose, but I wasn't that interested. The only subjects I did enjoy (apart from sport) were English, Religion and Drama. I remember the first three years of secondary school being extremely boring, with the only highlights being making Kung Fu stars in metalwork and dissecting a frog in biology.

Father Ian was a case; before he became a priest, he was the xylophone player in the band *The Tornados*, as well as a mad Celtic fan. He drank a lot, and we always used to find half empty whisky bottles in drawers in his office. The best thing about Father Ian was that he used to take me and my mate Damian to Reading Rock Festival in the summer, where we'd stay for three nights in a tent.

We actually assisted in the Christian tent, looking after drug addicts, winos, and other waifs and strays who needed help. This was when we were fourteen and fifteen, and it was a good age to see real life! The man in charge was called Pete, and he was huge – he was actually the head of a Hells Angels chapter. We would make tea, talk to the stoners, and generally help out in any way we could, and in return our eyes were opened to drugs, sex, alcohol, fighting... pretty much everything you can imagine going on at a rock festival. It was quite the experience.

The first time I went, the first main act on opening night was the *Sensational Alex Harvey Band*, who were just mind-blowing. Around this time, punk was just starting, and at those festivals I got my first look at young kids with Mohicans and ripped clothes. I didn't get any sleep for three days, but it was so worth it – I wouldn't have missed those two Reading trips for the world. Wow!

Back at school, Damian and I performed in a school talent competition, miming and dancing to two songs by our idol at the time, *Ziggy Stardust*, aka *David Bowie*. We did 'Suffragette City' and 'Lady Stardust'. Our make up and hair were top drawer and the kids loved it! So did I.

In my final year of school, I was asked to take the part of Sweeney Todd the Demon Barber in the end of year drama project, which I did without hesitation. It took three months to rehearse, and when it came to putting on the play, it was a sell-out. I thought I was good in the part of the lead, and so did several other people; my teacher told me that someone watching the play had suggested I go to drama school, something that she heartily agreed with. It was flattering but not what I wanted to do – after all, football was my number one passion, my dream.

I didn't do so well in my exams, however, and I didn't even turn up to some of them, knowing it was a lost cause. I got O Levels in English, Drama and RI, but that was it. I left Chatsmore at the age of sixteen and drifted around doing various different jobs, including working in a butchers shop and a shoe shop, being a golf caddy, and doing jobs on a building site.

I also joined Arundel football club at around this time, as my sports teacher played for them and had suggested I go along too. They were quite a good standard – they were in the County League – and I made good friends with the team while I was playing in the reserves. They actually adopted me in a way, teaching me how to drink and party.

One thing I noticed in the showers was that my cock was a lot bigger than average – in fact, it was bigger than most, if not all, of the team's. Once I realised this,

I started doing tricks with my penis, bringing it out at parties and so on. This became quite profitable in later years, but more of that later…

By seventeen, my body was forming well. I put my muscly legs down to playing football and the top half down to three years of my fabulous Bullworker, which I used all the time. It was around this time that I started stripping off regularly – I had a great body and I wasn't afraid to show it!

In October of my 17th year, I joined the Royal Navy, as I was starting to think about having a career. To start with, I really enjoyed the training, but when I went home for leave at Christmas, I had such a great time with my friends that I didn't want to go back to Plymouth. So, I went back, and because of my age, I took Premature Release. This meant that I didn't have to sign in for another five years.

Instead, I started working in a pub in Worthing called The Fountain. It was the perfect set up: all my friends hung out in there anyway, and I made loads of new friends from working there too. Even though Steve and I had sort of lost touch once I'd started playing for Arundel, I did see him sometimes during my time at the pub.

As well as Arundel, I also played for a Sunday side, Allington, which was again with my friends, and not as serious as when I played on Saturdays. At that time, my main team was Worthing under 18s, which was a great side and which had a brilliant manager in Jim Lelliot. We actually went on to win the Sussex under 18 league and cup final, as well as being relatively successful in the FA youth cup. At this point, Brighton Hove Albion asked me to come for training; we'd beaten their youth team three times that year, with me scoring in every single game against them. I was also training with Peter Ward, Gary Stevens and Stevee Foster around that time, all international players.

One Tuesday, I had a game against Aldershot Youth at Aldershot, where I scored two goals and played well. Ex-international Martin Chivers was in charge, and he even lent me his boots for the game. I got on really well with him, and we headed to the bar afterwards for a drink. Unfortunately, this turned into three or four pints, and the next morning, I was summoned to the office by the manager, Alan Mullery. I'd been seen drinking pints in the bar and he released me on the spot!

I still have Chivers' boots, though!

Chapter Two

In the summer of 1979, I went on a trip to the South of France with my friends Riv, Pete, Derek, Wakey, Beechy, Marin and Kevin – I knew this lot through both the pub and football. At seventeen, I was by far the youngest, with everyone else being around five to six years older.

All eight of us managed to squeeze into a transit van we'd hired for the journey, with three in the front and five in the back, plus tents, luggage, my Bullworker, and a bag containing shirts and shorts. There were also four crates of Kronenburg, the little bottles. Talk about being crammed in! There were no windows in the back of the van either, so you can imagine how cramped and claustrophobic it was.

We left from The Fountain on a Friday night in August, and we headed off to Newhaven to meet the midnight ferry. I had the ticket to Dieppe and about a tenner in cash.

Anyway, we got to the ferry and prepared for the five hour crossing. What do you do when you've got five hours to kill? Go to the bar, of course. There were a group of young women there, who I went right up to – I was extremely confident back then. It was a fun crossing; I had some good conversation and even ended up snogging a woman twice my age.

Eventually, we arrived at Dieppe (although we had another two hour wait before we could get off the boat), and it was hot and crammed on the journey to Paris. We got to the capital city late in the afternoon, and by that point the guys in the back of the van had almost been boiled alive – it was like a furnace back there.

Martin and Beechy were drinking a lot of beer, and I had the bright idea to go and get on top of the van, opening a bottle over the front. The beer spilled over Riv, the driver, who promptly stopped the van and gave me a stiff rebuke – as well as a boot up my arse! I wouldn't do that again. Needless to say, Riv was the sort of leader of the group, and what he said pretty much went.

After six hours of driving, it was beginning to get dark so we stopped the van and parked it on a grass verge at the side of a main road. We then got out our tent and pitched it next to the van so we could have a few hours' kip before we carried on down to St Raphael on the coast.

As it turns out, what we'd taken to be a grass verge in the darkness wasn't actually a grass verge at all – it was a police truck stop. Just our luck. Well, a policeman came over and woke us up, telling us he wasn't very happy about our sleeping there and asking us to get our tent and go. This wasn't an ideal situation at all, but I was just happy he hadn't thought to search the van – there was enough dope in there to get stoned for twenty years!

After this little detour, we finally got to the camp site and pitched up our two tents. I, however, didn't have a spot in either of these tents, or in the van – all I had was a mat on the ground and a sleeping bag, but it was good enough for me back then.

Just because I was away didn't stop me from doing my normal morning routine, which involved my usual Bullworker workout, much to the amusement of the others.

It was great. We swam, sunbathed and frolicked about all day, and although I never sorted out my own food for my meals, I got by on picking scraps of uneaten food off people's plates.

The holiday also, of course, involved women. For instance, Derek – the suave, handsome estate agent – was his usual charming self and managed to pull a stunning bird on just our second night there. She was about twenty years old, Italian, with long, black hair and a lovely body. They spoke for a while and then I saw them slide off from the bar and walk away from the others, heading back to the campsite. I followed them as they went into the van, and when I sneaked into the back, I found them shagging. They knew I was there and they didn't seem to mind this unexpected bit of voyeurism. In fact, once Derek had finished and got off, the beauty beckoned me over and asked me to shag her too. Fantastic! I rammed her and she loved it, but when I was done, she still wanted more. Riv popped his head in the van for a bit, and I left them to it as I walked over to Juppy's tent. He was polaxed drunk, but I woke him and walked him over to the van. By this point, the woman was ready for another, so Pete lay on top of her while I helped him manoeuvre in his drunk state, pushing his arse in and out until he finished. Well, what are mates for?

It was one hell of a crazy night, that's for sure, and I went back to my mat on the ground giggling to myself. We never saw the woman again.

After a week, Derek had to get home, and as I had no money left, I decided to join him on the train back. I bunked it all the way to Dieppe, where Del paid for my ferry ticket back to England.

I enjoyed working in the pub, but I also worked for an industrial cleaning firm in the early mornings to make some more money. Me and some of my friends (my main crew) met up every Friday in a pub called the Elms, and we called ourselves 'the Committee'. This consisted of myself, Paul, Dizzy, Sloggett, Jono, Yanto and Sirius. We'd have a few beers and a few lines of speed and then we'd be off to Brighton in Sloggett's Dad's camper van. Once we were there, we'd meet up with Andy Faggot and Warwick in the Electric Grape and then go on to the Inn Place. This was an underground cellar, and although it was small, it was amazing. It played host to all sorts – rockabillies, goths, skinheads, new romantics and more – but there was never any trouble.

The last song they always played there every night was 'Shout' by Lulu, which always caused mayhem in the small venue. By this time of night, my quiff would have inevitably started to droop, and I had a pretty amazing quiff back then, so that's saying something.

There would always be a few birds up for it at the Inn Place, and we'd often head back to Paul's house afterwards with some girls from the bar. In fact, quite often, me, Paul and Jono would go there and have sex with Nat, a pretty little punk girl.

I always looked forward to those nights.

* * *

In the summer of 1980, I went to America. I was just 18 years old and I'd managed to get a visa by doctoring my bank account statement. I personally went to the American Embassy to get it, along with Riv, little Kevin, and Mandy – a girl we'd met the previous year during our South of France trip.

We decided to go to Miami, even though two weeks earlier there had been big riots in the city – not a very nice atmosphere to go into.

We flew on a Freddie Laker sky train ticket, and it cost me just £50 for my single ticket to Miami. A little different compared to these days.

I travelled light; I had a small holdall with some clothes, and a sausage sandwich which my dad had packed for me. That was the only thing I was carrying as I went through the airport security.

Once we were through and had boarded the plane (which was a massive jumbo), we flew off to America. I was really excited, and after 10 hours, we landed in Miami. I didn't know what I'd been expecting, but it was so much better than I could have imagined. I could see the lights of the city through the window as we landed, and from the air, it looked amazing.

Once we'd got off the plane, we passed through immigration, where I told them I was leaving America from a different city, as I only had a single ticket.

Finally, we were in the USA.

We got a taxi downtown to a hotel we'd pre-booked back in England, and we planned to stay there for a fortnight before heading to Nassau in the Bahamas. When we were there, the plan was to get a permit so we could work on the TSS Festival, a cruise ship which sailed around the Caribbean. My friends had worked on this ship before and I couldn't wait to join too.

While we were in Miami, I lounged around the pool and swam in the ocean – it was great. I made friends with one of the lifeguards at the hotel and he took me out on his parents' boat. From this boat, we went fishing and snorkelling, which was pretty surreal; it was completely different to what I was used to back in England.

After two weeks of being in Miami, I decided I didn't want to go to Nassau after all; my money was rapidly running out and I wasn't sure I'd even get a job on the cruise ship. So, instead of forking out money for the flight to Nassau, I left my friends and decided to go to Houston instead, as my Mum's sister lived there – I thought I'd go and look her up.

My aunt's name was Margarette, and she'd met Clark – an American GI – during the war. Clark had brought her back to America with him, where they married and settled down in Pasadena, a suburb of Houston.

I had just enough money for a greyhound ticket to Texas, and so I set off on my own, with no more than an address and a phone number for once I got to Pasadena.

The journey took two days, and during these long hours of travelling, the coach stopped regularly. On one of these stops, I got off the coach for an hour to walk around and stretch my legs, and when I got back on, I noticed that my bag – which had been under my seat – had disappeared. Some of the passengers had got off the coach at this stop, and it was clear that one of the shitheads had stolen it. I searched the whole coach and asked the driver for help, but there was nothing I could do about it. I was so angry.

That evening, the coach arrived in Houston and I rang Margarette – luckily, I had her number on me when my bag 'went missing' – and she came and got me before driving me back to her house, which was about thirty minutes from the bus station.

I had nothing, just the clothes on my back, but luckily, Margarette's son was near my age, so I got to borrow some of his not-so-trendy gear. It was better than nothing.

I thought that while I was there I'd have a look at the local football (or soccer as they call it over there), so I headed over to the training grounds of the Houston Astros. I told them I played for Brighton & Hove Albion in England and managed to train with them for a couple of days. They wouldn't sign me, however.

Margarette's husband Clark was almost retired, but he still had a job delivering products to hardware stores all over Texas, and I helped him out some days, which kept me busy for a while.

One incident from my time in America that I'll never forget concerned Margarette's neighbours, or more specifically, the neighbours' daughter. As she was around the same age as me, I was invited over one hot, sunny afternoon, and when I knocked on the door, the daughter answered, a plump, pretty girl about 18 years old. She asked me inside, and before I'd even said anything to her, she looked at me and informed me, "I've never had a British cock before so I want you to fuck me, babe."

Of course, being the polite Englishman I was, I obliged and rammed her on the floor hard. Afterwards, she said, "Wow baby, I needed that," handed me a lemonade, and announced she was off to softball. She asked if I wanted to join her but I politely refused. Now, I'd heard that Americans liked an English accent, and they do, but I'd never thought something like that would happen quite so quickly – it was easier than I would have ever thought possible.

By this point, I had no money, no clothes and no work, so I decided to go home. I suppose I could have stayed in Houston for a bit longer, but I felt ready to leave.

This wasn't going to be as easy as I'd hoped, however, as my passport had been in the bag that was stolen from the bus, and when Margarette gave me a lift to the British Consulate in Houston, she said goodbye and left me there. She was under the impression that they'd be able to help me out straight away, and so was I, but it didn't quite happen like that.

They did help me with my problem, but not before they'd banged me up in a holding cell for two nights with some unfriendly Mexicans. It wasn't a great time. Finally, though, I was sent home in a mail plane and charged with vagrancy.

I got back to England safe and sound, with a hundred new memories from my interesting time in the USA.

* * *

From the ages of 19 to 22, I played football for Littlehampton and Steyning. I actually used to work for the chairman, Barry Wadsworth, who owned a few greengrocer shops; three mornings a week, we'd set off at four in the morning to the fruit and vegetables market at Covent Garden. During this time, I also worked with my friend Jono on several building sites in Haywards Heath. I absolutely lived for the weekends, and come Friday afternoon, it was party time.

I had a bit of a routine going. As soon as I got paid, I'd buy a Chevignon shirt – or some other classy bit of cloth – and then the rest of my wages were spent on having a good time over the weekend, mainly going on drink, drugs and clubs. By Sunday night I would always be completely penniless and ready to get a sub at work the next morning.

After a wild Friday night, I'd have football on the Saturday, and after that was finished, I'd meet up with the lads and head off to Brighton for yet another heavy night at The Escape Club or Subterfuge.

It wasn't all fun and games at this age, however. In the winter of 1981, I had appendicitis. Although this was pretty routine, my wound got infected, so a week after coming out of the hospital, I was rushed back in, with a ball the size of a tennis ball on my stitches. The doctor – who had no time to be gentle – had to pierce it, something which was so painful that I remember it vividly to this day.

I stayed in the hospital for a couple of days after that and then was back out, luckily with no lasting damage. There was a plus to all this, however – I ended up shagging the nurse who was there whilst I was getting stabbed!

A couple of days after this, I went up the Findon Gallops with some friends, and at the top there's a path that's both steep and wide. As it was snowing, there were plenty of people there, tobogganing and having a great time, despite the freezing weather. There was me, Paul, Jono, Gigg and a few more, and someone had brought (or dumped) an old car bonnet there – perfect for tobogganing, I thought. Well, no one else would dare use it, but I had no intention of letting the opportunity go. I stripped off naked, lay on the bonnet, and shouted, "Push!"

Immediately, all of the people milling around got out of my way, and my friends pushed me down the slope. Boy, did I go fast! I ended up at the fence at the bottom of the field, and happily walked back up the hill to my friends. Some people cheered me on the way back up, while others expressed their opinions of me being a 'nutter'. The parents were definitely not amused, but I had a great time. When I got back to the top, I got dressed and made a quick exit.

The whole thing had been fun, but it hadn't been the best thing for my stitches.

* * *

Another holiday I remember well was my trip to Greece in the summer of 82 (a World Cup year). It was me, Perry, Daryl, Sloggett and Stenty, and while Stenty and I went on the train, the others took the Magic Bus, going a day before me.

Stenty wasn't one of our good friends – we knew him from the pub and football – but he'd heard about the trip and asked if he could tag along. He was a boxer and a bit of a looney. Anyway, we set off from Victoria on our three day trip to Athens, where we'd arranged to meet the others by the main statue in Syntagma Square.

Stenty and I got to Paris via a ferry crossing, and it was here that he started drinking. Now, drinking with Stenty was an interesting experience to say the least. For instance, he would always carry a small, furry toy monkey in his pocket, and whenever he was on the booze, he'd get it out and start talking to it. He'd annoy absolutely everyone around him by doing this, and it happened a lot during that trip.

From Paris, we joined another train to Venice, getting there in the early morning. We had five hours to kill until our connection, and while I wanted to walk around a bit and check out St Peter's Square, Stenty had other ideas.

He had no desire to sightsee, instead buying two gallons of wine, which he planned on drinking in the park near the station. I left him to it and went and took in the sights.

When I got back to the station a few hours later, I saw a crowd of people surrounding a figure. This man was dancing and shouting and tossing something up into the air – a toy monkey. I just about managed to drag Stenty away before he could get arrested, and then we got on our train.

The next stop was Trieste, a city on the Italian Yugoslav border, and this would take us down through Belgrade to Thessaloniki, Greece. We got into a small train carriage, with more than ten people crammed in together. Four of these people were a mean-looking lot, and I silently prayed that Stenty wasn't going to start shadow boxing with them or anything. Luckily, he crashed out, and I managed to get along with the four people, who were from Yugoslavia – I swapped fags and food with them. After a while, Stenty woke up and joined us, and luckily, they thought Stenty was funny rather than annoying.

After some more talking and laughing, they asked us if we wouldn't mind carrying two holdalls through the station at Belgrade for them; they said they couldn't carry them through without being stopped. We agreed to help, although there wasn't much else we could have done under the circumstances – I felt we weren't really being given a choice in the matter.

Stenty and I looked like typical holidaymakers, especially Stenty, who was wearing a Union Jack t-shirt. Anyway, we all got off at Belgrade and we took one of their holdalls each, along with our other bags. We followed the Yugoslavs out of the station and headed across the road to a café, where we sat down and had a drink. When we got up, we left the holdalls behind, and the Yugoslavs slyly waved as we headed back to the station.

Coffee smuggling! We were relieved; I wasn't sure what was going to happen if we got caught, but at least we didn't have to find out.

After this, we set off for another twelve hour train journey to Thessaloniki, and when we got there, we stepped off the train for a few hours before boarding another one to Athens. This one was absolutely packed and we had to stand the whole way.

We eventually got to Athens at midday on Day Three of our journey. We were completely knackered, but we headed over to Syntagma Square to meet our friends. There was no sign of them. We were a few hours late, but I thought they would have hung around to meet us. Apparently not. Of course, back in those days there were no mobiles, no tablets and no way of communicating if you didn't meet up at the time and place you'd agreed on. You don't realise how stuck for communication you are without modern technology – a nightmare.

We were just about to give up and go and look for a hostel when I heard someone shouting my name – well, my nickname: "Woody!!!" Relieved, we met the boys, embraced, and then went back to the hostel they'd already booked into.

The next day we spent sightseeing around Athens, and then we decided to go to Crete. It was a 6 p.m. ferry with a twelve hour crossing time, and after we got on the underground to Pireaus, we boarded, excited. The crossing wasn't too bad – we had a few beers and then slept. After we got off the ferry in Heraklion, the next leg of our journey was a bus to Malia, and then onto a campsite about twenty miles to the east of Heraklion.

We pitched up and stayed there for a few weeks doing the usual: swimming, sunbathing, shagging and drinking. Stenty did plenty of the latter, and we lost him a few weeks into the trip as he didn't want to go island hopping like the rest of us.

After Stenty left, we went to the island of Ios, the Ibiza of the 80s! We found a nice campsite there on one of the beaches, and the location was fantastic. It had everything we needed or could possibly want; so many clubs and bars and birds it was incredible.

From Ios we went on a trip to Sikinos, a small island about three hours' sailing from Ios. We didn't know much about the island, but we were disappointed to find that there wasn't much there – it had one taverna and one shop (both the same building) in the port and one town up at the top of a hill, about three miles away. It was incredibly small, quiet, and pretty much deserted. Due to this, we decided to spend just one night on the beach before going on to another island.

In the taverna, the owner told us that not many people went there, apart from for archaeological trips – fossil hunters and the like. He also told us that you could only get to the town at the top of the hill by a dirt track. As it wasn't a proper road, only donkeys or jeeps were allowed – no cars.

Even though it was 100 degree heat, we decided to go up there, and it was quite some trek – we didn't get up until about 6 p.m. The locals all stared at us like we were aliens; obviously, they didn't get many visitors, and the fact that we all had cropped, dyed blond hair probably didn't help. There wasn't much in the town, either, just a couple of shops for food and another taverna. Of course, we headed straight for it, and it was there that we had the most beautiful meal of fish and moussaka I'd ever had. In fact, it still hasn't been bettered to this day, not in my mind. After we'd eaten, we headed back down to the beach, our way lit only by the moon and stars. It was a good evening, and one I remember well.

We slept on the beach with no problems, but as the night went on, we noticed the wind was getting stronger and stronger, and when we were ready to leave the next day, we headed over to the port, only to be told by the taverna/shop owner that there wouldn't be a ferry at all that day – it was too windy.

Shit. This wasn't what we wanted to hear, and we went back to the beach. That day I accidentally dropped a five drachmas note in the sea, and as I was short for money, I spent hours swimming and snorkelling in the hope of getting it back. I didn't.

One person was happy in all of this, however: the shop owner. As he was the only option at the port, we had to buy our food from him, and the only things he had to offer were bread, eggs and giant tomatoes. We had a small primer so we could heat up the eggs, and once we'd hollowed out the bread and filled the hole in with eggs and tomatoes, we had a pretty decent big sandwich. However, after three days of eating this, it got a little repetitive.

The three days eventually passed and we managed to get back to Ios, the only route out from Sikinos, where we stayed for another week or so. I remember coming into the port, listening to a Mary Wilson tune on Gigg's Walkman and thinking how stunning it was – the views were amazing. We managed to find a beach to crash on and then headed over to a taverna, which was playing Italy vs West Germany, the World Cup Final. The end result was 3-1 Italy, and it was a great night.

Unfortunately, soon after we realised we had to leave the island and head back to Crete, as money was going fast and we desperately needed to find some work. I phoned my brother asking for help and he telexed through £100, "and no more!" as he'd told me. It helped, but I still needed cash, and we came up with a rather ingenious way of raising some extra money.

The idea was this. In evenings at bars near the campsites, I would wear a robe, and Perry would wrap a towel around my head, draping fruit (such as bananas etc.) from it. I'd start dancing in front of the packed bars and then take my robe and shorts off, ready to unleash my party trick on the unsuspecting crowd. I used to put ten small drachma coins behind my foreskin, and plop them out one by one. Then I would tie my cock nearly into a knot, and when I jiggled, it would slowly unravel, much to the amusement of the crowd. Perry would then go round with a cap and collect money from the audience – a nice little earner. Of course, we had to run off before the police turned up, as weirdly, Greeks didn't like that sort of thing.

I had another job when I was there, something a little less glamorous. You see, the toilets there are stand up ones, and people often missed. It was my job to push the shit down in the toilets, where it was meant to go – so gross!

Sloggett got some work with a builder, and then me, Daryl and Perry got a job clearing fields for banana plantations. For this, we'd get picked up in a three wheeler truck, and when we got there, we'd have to load rocks at the end of the field, before helping load them onto bulldozers. Lunch was pretty good with that job – we'd have bread, olives and cheese, washed down with retsina, a very strong local wine. It was so strong, in fact, that after one small bottle of it, we were pissed. This didn't bode well for the afternoons of work.

One day, it was extremely hot and Perry and I were dropping rocks into the bucket of a dozer. They were so heavy that we had to throw them in double handed. Unfortunately, while I was in the middle of doing this, I tripped, just as I was throwing a particularly huge rock in. Perry's hand was on the metal blade and as I dropped it onto his hand, one of his fingers just... exploded. There isn't any other word for it. It really wasn't a pretty sight, and he got rushed to hospital. After that, there was no more work for either of us at that job, mainly because of what happened on the way back from the hospital. We were getting a lift to the field in the back of a JCB, and I accidentally pushed something, which caused the bucket to drop and which ended in ten yards of Tarmac being gouged out of the road – oops.

Soon after, Sloggs got short changed by his builder so he finished working there, and we had to stop him from doing something stupid; I'm sure the police wouldn't take it lightly if the builder had been beaten up.

We had to wait a week or so for Perry's hand to heal, and during this time we met a traveller who took us up to the mountains to get work grape picking in the village of Tillisos. We met our potential new employers in the local tavern and soon, me, Daryl and Perry had been taken on by an eighty-year-old farmer. He said we could stay at his house and sleep on the roof. Sloggett, however, wasn't very keen on this arrangement, and as he had a job waiting for him at Dicky Dirts clothes shop in Soho, he decided to head home.

The farmer was a nice man and we would follow him to his field on the local transport system – donkeys. We worked really long hours, and how I kept up I'll never know. His brothers were older and still working, though, so I felt like I couldn't give up. After three weeks, we'd picked everything, and the work was coming to an end. We needed to decide what we were doing next.

Daryl and Perry wanted to go to Rhodes but I wanted to see my brother in The Hague in Holland. So, we said our goodbyes in Heraklion and I got on a Magic Bus. I realised that with the route the bus took, we'd go past Schladming in the Alps – my mother's home town – and I asked the driver if he'd be able to let me off near it. He agreed, and about 36 hours into the drive, I hopped out on the autobahn, two miles from Schladming.

It was in the early hours, it was October, and it was getting colder – the walk to the town wasn't as pleasant as it could have been. I didn't really know where I was going, but I had an address and phone number for my mum's friend, Mina, who I hoped would help me out.

As it was still dark when I got there, I slept in a bus shelter for a couple of hours, and when it was light, I called Mina. She came and got me before taking me to my mother's house, where I was met by Uncle Naz, my mum's brother. We hugged and had some coffee before he went off to work; a big man, Naz was employed on the big mountain above Schladming called the Dachstein. He loved his job, and he loved a drink (or several). We got on well.

Mina prepared a room for me in this big house and I was delighted to find a big bed with a large, comfy continental quilt. I lay my head down on the soft pillow and slept for hours.

I stayed there for a week, meeting a lot of people during that time, as Mina introduced me to several men and women around my age. She also introduced me to someone else. One day, she took me off up a dirt track which ended with a cabin by the river. Not quite knowing what we were doing there, I stood with baited breath while Mina knocked on the door.

Before long, the door opened to reveal an older gentleman with an absolutely massive moustache. He took one look at me and started shouting, "Rudi! Rudi!"

I was stunned. Who was this guy?

Soon, however, Mina explained the situation to me and it all became clear.

This man was my granddad, who I'd never met and who I didn't know was still alive. Obviously, I knew my mum must have had a father, but she'd never told me anything about him, not once!

It turned out that my mum was born out of wedlock, meaning that she was ostracised, and was brought up by her mum and the father of Naz, who was younger. I wished my mum had told me about him, but I understand that she had her reasons for not doing so.

It was strange to see this place, belonging to a man I didn't know existed, and with photos of me on the wall! To think those pictures had been there for years and I'd had no idea – it was bizarre to say the least.

What happened next was even stranger. I was asked to sit down and then I watched as my granddad took out an accordion – his 'squeeze box' – and started playing. He yodelled at the same time, and although he was good, it was a pretty hilarious sight to see. He also tried to give me gifts, ones I couldn't accept. For instance, he wanted to give me a Luger (a German pistol) and an old haunting rifle, among other things. I politely declined all of them and had a glass of wine instead.

After a few more minutes and another hug, I left. That was both the first and the last time I would ever see him – extremely surreal. Still, I had plans to meet up with my brother in Holland and so I said goodbye and Mina took me to the train station.

There's a lot I could say about my brother Richard, but here are the basics.

When I went to visit him, he was living in The Hague, working as an interpreter and engineer for some big Dutch company. He had gained a degree at the Imperial College London (while I got honours in pulling birds and kicking a football around) and could speak both German and Dutch, hence his job.

I arrived in The Hague in the morning and found Richard's place – a nice flat where he lived with his girlfriend. We had a good time, going for walks and having meals in nice restaurants, but I didn't feel totally comfortable there. For one thing, Richard had told his girlfriend that Dad was dead – he wasn't, but I suppose that to my brother, he was; they didn't exactly have the best of relationships.

When I was ready to leave, Richard bought me a ticket from Hook of Holland to Harwich, another ten hour ferry crossing. When I eventually got back to Worthing, I was completely skint, but I had memories of a very interesting summer to make up for it.

I was never really close with Richard, but all that changed during the last three years of his life, when I helped care for him. When he moved back to England, he got another degree and did some more work. He never married, and soon he became depressed and then very ill. It turned out he had a rare condition called MSM – a Multiple System Atrophy. This means that the body literally starts to shut down, very slowly, dragging it out for the poor sufferer. Soon he was confined to a wheelchair and I used to visit him at weekends, taking him places to get him out of the house.

It was hard to see him like that, so different to how he was when he was younger. He was an extremely intelligent man, and he had a very dry humour. When he was a child, our dad was brutal to him; Richard suffered very badly from acne when he was a teenager and was very self-conscious about it, something which Dad didn't help with at all – he would constantly take the mick out of him because of it and even physically abuse him.

When he got a little older and the acne disappeared, Richard became handsome and was quite a hit with the ladies. Even though he didn't need to, he would pay for prostitutes to visit him in his converted flat. Well, actually, I was the one who organised them for him, two at a time sometimes. It wasn't so bad – I used to get a free go.

I was with him in the hospital during his last days, and I watched his last breath with a mixture of feelings – sorrow, but also some relief; he was finally out of torment and off to another realm.

Chapter Three

I met my first girlfriend, Ally, at the Inn Place in Brighton.

She was originally from Worthing but lived in London, where she worked for Steve Strange, the pop star and New Romantic. Her parents were still in the area and so she would come down some weekends to see them, as well as her mates. She used to stay at her friend Kim's house, a hairdresser she'd known for years. I used to stay over at Kim's house with Ally, and soon we started our relationship.

When in London, Ally lived with a couple of flat share mates in Camden Town. This was really handy for me as she used to get me and all of my mates into the Camden Palace on Tuesday nights – the Palace's biggest evening of the week. One night we saw *Madonna*, and we also saw *King* play, my favourite band. As well as going to the Palace, we used to get on the guest list of the Wag Club and Le Beat Route in Soho. We had some mad times back then, drinking, taking drugs, getting no sleep, going to all these clubs... amazing. Some crazy things happened. For instance, *Marilyn* – the blonde, gay, male singer – was one of Ally's friends and used to stay at the flat sometimes, and one day, Ally got me in as a dancer in the *Wham* video for 'Bad Boys'. You couldn't see much of me in it, but it was fun nonetheless.

In the summer of 82 I got a job with the council, looking after Tarring tennis and bowls club as an attendant. I had an office where people would come in and pay for the tennis courts, and I also had to look after the bowling club bowlers. There were two courts and one small, green hideaway.

Daryl worked with me in a shift system, seven days a week in the summer with a shift pattern of 9-3 or 3-9. I didn't mind it, though – in fact, I loved the job. We made friends with the local kids, and because of this, I'm sure we stopped a lot of vandalism and graffiti from appearing in the vicinity. As well as the kids, the elderly gentlemen and ladies of the bowls club liked us too, and there were some really great characters amongst them.

Another reason I loved my job was because I could be a bit sneaky. For instance, it cost £1.35 an hour to hire a court, but when any foreign students came along, we charged them that each. So, I used to make a bit of money on the side. My mates would also come and play – we all had a bit of a league going on. As far as work went, it was pretty fun. The boss liked us, too; he played there and seemed to appreciate the way we stopped the vandalism and graffiti.

After a while, Ally became ill with glandular fever and had to come back to Worthing to live with her parents – she needed to get well and have a break from her hectic lifestyle, which had clearly got the better of her.

One morning, after a shift at the tennis courts, I went round to see her at her parents' house. I remember it was a really hot day, and Ally told me her parents were out with her grandparents. Liking the fact that we had the place to ourselves, we sat on the couch to have a cuppa, and after a few minutes, she told me to take my shorts off – I was in for a treat!

I lay down on the couch and let Ally get on with the sucking, making me hard very quickly. I kept hearing noises but Ally kept insisting that we were alone, so I let it go. Just before I shot, however, the door – which I was facing – slammed open and her mum appeared, looking at me straight in the eyes as Ally was still going for it.

"I thought they were out!" I said, panicked, as Ally looked up at me. She said that they were meant to be. Shit! I needed to go, but Ally told me not to worry – it was just an accident.

I wasn't, however, going to stick around after that, so I quickly jumped off the couch and pulled my shorts up, prick now down and away.

Then it hit me: the only way out was through the kitchen, and they were all in it – her parents and her grandparents! Shit. Those were the longest six steps I'd ever taken, and I shyly winced and mumbled my goodbyes as I let myself out.

Fuck, that was hot.

I ran and ran all the way home.

* * *

Ally and I soon moved into a flat of our own in Worthing high street. It was on the top floor with a shoe shop (Freeman Hardy Willis) and a hairdressers (Uneedus) below, and we got the room thanks to my friend, Dave. Dave was a guru type, a man who sported a big beard and who liked his dope. He worked as an assistant in a top trendy clothes shop, Squires, and used to do a bit of chippy work as well. Lorraine and Bob also lived there – a couple about eight years older than us.

Our room looked down on the high street, and it was special in that it had carpeted walls – weird but different – apart from the main wall of the front room, which was just a massive poster of a Caribbean beach. The flat was big and was a lot like a coffee shop, with people always popping round, day or night. Ally got a job in a boutique, which suited her perfectly, but soon, there was another opportunity for us to earn money – this time together.

Basically, a good friend of ours asked if we wanted to do some modelling at a big clothes show for several shops in Brighton. We thought it sounded fun so we agreed – I was to model boxer shorts while Ally modelled some dresses. It was a pretty big deal; it was going to be held at The Pink Coconut (a big club) in Brighton, and several local dignitaries would be in the audience, including the mayor. We couldn't really miss the opportunity.

Anyway, we went over on the morning of the show for the rehearsals, and we were to stay there all day until the actual show itself, which started at 8 p.m.

My outfit was a pair of tight boxers and a robe, and during the rehearsal, we found out our routines. My part in the show involved sitting at a table with two other models, chatting and sipping our wine until we got our cue, which was 'Let's Dance' by *David Bowie*. At this point, we were to stand up one by one and walk one at a time to the front of the stage. Here we would pose, de-robe, and then strut back to the table. It sounded pretty simple to me, but that was before the drinking started.

The boys and girls were separated for the show, meaning I was left alone with the other male models while Ally was left with the girls. Perhaps if we'd been able to stay together, what happened next might have been a little different.

We had about two hours to kill before the show started, and as there wasn't much to do, I started drinking and having a laugh with the other models. I had perhaps a little more than I should have done.

The fact that the mayor was going to be at the show didn't stop me from having more booze, and neither did the fact that Ally's family would be in the audience – her parents and her grandparents.

The club was packed – around 900 people in total – and I was wasted. Oops.

Well, the show started and the models came on in all sorts of clothes, doing their thing and getting cheers and applause from the crowd. I watched and waited for my turn, which was in the second half.

Eventually, the curtains opened after the break and it was show time. I sat with my model friends at the table, chatting and sipping our drinks – well, I was glugging mine more than anything.

Before I knew it, 'Let's Dance' started blaring out of the speakers and the first model was up and doing his thing. When it was my turn, I stood up, a little wobbly it has to be said, and made my way to the front of the stage, just about getting there without falling over.

When I got there, I noticed about eight of my friends at the front of the crowd, and forgetting about everyone else who was in the audience, I focused on them, smiling my drunken smile as I clumsily took off my robe.

"Woody, get 'em off!" shouted one of my friends, and in my intoxicated state, I thought this was a brilliant idea. So, without wasting another second, I took my boxers off and threw them into the crowd with a drunken flourish. I didn't stop there, either. I was really getting into the music by now and I thought it would be a great idea to start gyrating on the stage and swinging my cock around.

Well, the event promoters didn't like that, and before I knew it, the main lights had come on and I was being manhandled from the stage. They just gave me enough time to grab my clothes from the dressing room and then I was escorted outside.

When Ally got back later on that night, I got a serious beating, not to mention the stick I got from her (and my mates) for months afterwards.

It wasn't long after this that the inevitable happened. I went for a 'quiet drink' one Friday and ended up getting hijacked by my friends. We ended up at a nurse's party and when I finally got back home on the Sunday morning, I found that Ally had left me.

All her stuff was gone, and all her clothes had vanished from the wardrobe – that was it: it was over. I was upset at the time, as we had some fun, but I understand why she left.

Ally eventually moved to America and I was so sad to hear that she died about three years ago. She left behind two kids. Rest in Peace, Ally.

* * *

After that, there was a big change around at the flat; Bob and Lorraine moved to Australia and my mate Swads moved in in their place. He was a manager of Knowls Bakery in Crawley, and a goalkeeper as well – not a great one, it has to be said, but he played for the reserves at Wick. He was a good guy, although he loved carp fishing and regularly boiled up his bait in our kitchen, which used to smell awful for hours afterwards.

We'd go out a lot together for drinks and stuff, and one night we brought a bird back from the pub – she was keen and she wanted us both to fuck her. We were all up for it, and so we got in my bed. I lay next to them as Swads started shagging her, and it was the weirdest thing I'd ever heard in my life; just as he was about to cum, he started making the most bizarre screaming sounds – not normal noises at all.

I looked at the girl and she looked at me, with a sort of 'What the fuck was that?' expression on her face. Well, that was it. I had to get out of there – I was laughing too much. I ran out and left them to it, laughing the whole time. Of course, I told all of my mates about it immediately. What an embarrassing orgasm, what a knob!

Around that time of my life, I hit it hard, doing drugs, drinking, and going to lots and lots of clubs. The weekends were all the same – a wild blur of parties and forgotten memories.

One Sunday morning, after a particularly heavy night, I woke up as I was getting a nice blowjob. I couldn't remember who I'd pulled the night before – was it the woman from the bar or the woman from the club? But as I pulled back the sheets, I couldn't believe what I was seeing. It wasn't a woman at all; it was Andy Faggot! No!

Andy looked up at me, smiled, said, "Thanks Woody, I've always loved you," then jumped up and ran out. It was a little surreal, but I made sure I told all of my friends before Andy did – you should always get in first with these kinds of things.

Because of my wild weekends, my football had started to suffer a bit, but I soon got it back on course when I joined Steyning, the county league side. It helped that the manager there – Barry Youel – knew my family; his dad and my dad were lifelong friends, and he sort of forced me to join. As well as managing the team, he owned a few butcher shops, and he was a big man with an even bigger reputation. In fact, he was a bit of a scary customer.

Basically, he wanted to win the league, he wanted to form a great side, and he wanted me as a striker. He was determined to get what he wanted and he was extremely persuasive – he gave me good money, drugs, and meat from his shops (I'd always give the meat to my mum).

Due to his determination, we became a good side and we got to the quarter finals of the FA Vase, which was a huge achievement. We also won the county league that season as well – the first time in their history. I was proud to be part of that team.

At the same time, I was also playing for Sussex, but I was still managing to go out and do crazy things around my footballing commitments. For instance, I once ate a small bit of Jono's shit wrapped up in tissue for a bet, and I loved to streak everywhere; I even walked into M&S and asked if they could assist me in buying a suit, while I was stark naked. Another thing I would do on a semi-regular basis was to put lit cigarettes up my arse – totally weird and crazy stuff that started to become quite regular. Magic mushrooms were one of my favourites, as I always used to see the weirdest things. For instance, one day, after a cup of mushrooms, I went to the supermarket and watched my hair grow several feet until I was tripping over it!

I still loved weekends and got plenty of shagging in, but there was one woman who always stood out to me. I used to see her walking along the street opposite my flat every evening at around six o'clock, and she was beautiful, with long, black hair and a stunning face. After a while of seeing her near where I lived, I ran into her at Rhapsody's Wine Bar, where she was working. Of course, I just had to ask her out, and I was happy when she said yes.

Her name was Sarah and she was a bit younger than me and incredibly posh, but we went for a few drinks and a couple of meals, and we got on really well. I played it cool and after about five to six weeks I got her in bed – bingo! This felt different to a lot of the random women I'd had in my bed at weekends, though, and I really liked Sarah; she was good fun. So, we decided to make it official that we were going out with each other. Incidentally, it was Sarah's grandmother who I found myself having a little kissing session with on her 80th birthday, but the less said about that the better.

Back at the flat, we found out it was going to be turned into offices and that we'd have a couple of months there at the most before we had to leave. Everyone was a bit sad by this situation, but Dave in particular was devastated. He didn't want to leave, and he didn't actually leave when he was supposed to; he squatted in the empty flat for two months before the building work started, living without any electricity or gas.

Luckily, Jono had just bought a two bedroom flat in East Worthing and he said I could move in with him. It was actually a really nice flat and in a great location, just one hundred yards from the beach.

By this point, I'd started working for Carl Stabler, a concrete and floor specialist, and I used to cycle to my job every day from East Worthing to Littlehampton – which is about a 24 mile round trip. The job was doing all the concrete finishing at the new Body Shop headquarters, and I'd got it because of my football associations. I'd just joined Wick from Steyning (the new chairman was Barry Wadsworth, the old Littlehampton chairman), and as Carl's dad was vice chairman at Wick, the job automatically became mine when I joined.

One incident from around this time that I'll always remember happened at Jono's flat, where I was living at the time. It concerned Jono's ex, who was the mother of his two kids, and who obviously wasn't coping very well. She rang the flat in the early hours and I answered. At first, I couldn't make out who it was or what she was saying, as the woman on the end of the phone was hysterical, but then I recognised Helen's voice. She'd heard about Jono's new girlfriend and was completely distraught about the whole thing. As she wasn't making any sense, and as she wasn't listening to anything I was saying, I put the phone down, thinking that would be the end of it.

I was wrong. About an hour later, I was woken by the sound of smashing glass. Still a little dazed, I came out of my room to find Helen running to the kitchen and grabbing a knife out of the block – a big one. I took in the devastation and realised she'd smashed through the glass panel in our front door to get in.

I quickly woke up after that, and I ran towards Helen, grabbing the knife out of her hand as fast as I could. In fact, it was so fast that I ended up cutting my own hand in the process.

Jono was awake at this point – how could he not be after the racket Helen was making? – but he refused to come out of his room. I didn't blame the guy. I was just glad that neither Jono's girlfriend nor my girlfriend were staying over that night, or it could have been a lot worse.

I managed to keep hold of Helen with a bear hug while Jono called the police, and soon they arrived and took her away. It was clear that she'd completely flipped, and she was kept overnight at the police station. The next morning, Jono had to go down to the station to sort things out. She was cautioned and told to stay away from him.

Shortly afterwards, Jono bought a three bedroom Victorian town house in central Worthing and I moved with him.

Chapter Four

Another holiday that sticks in my mind is a skiing holiday I went on in the Italian Alps.

It sounds idyllic, but it was anything but.

It was me, my girlfriend Sarah, Jono, Jono's girlfriend Sarah, Jono's sister Sheena and Jupp Steve, who was older than us and quite a character. I'd never been skiing before and I was looking forward to it.

It didn't start well. When it was time to board the plane, I realised I must have left mine and Sarah's flight bags in the car, and when I went back to get them, they were nowhere to be found – oops. I was rummaging everywhere, frantically trying to find them before our plane left, but it was no good, and we simply had to board. At the last minute, however, a security guard waved us over and showed us our bags. It was a huge relief, but we were only just allowed to board, and Sarah was crying as we ran to the departure gate. Not the best start to a holiday.

It didn't get much better after that. When we arrived at Milan, I got stopped at passport control because of the deportation stamp I had in there from the USA. It wasn't just someone asking me a question, either; they actually took me into a room at gunpoint and grilled me for what seemed like forever.

I was only just let out in time to get the coach to the hotel, and because of my detainment, the coach had been delayed – let's just say I wasn't exactly popular when I finally took my seat. Because of this, Sarah was crying again.

The coach trip itself was frightening. We were on a very narrow road as we made our way up into the Alps, and there was ice on the ground and fog in the air. We were just feet away from the edge of the road, which fell down at a very steep angle – a guaranteed icy death if we were to plunge off it. Everyone on the coach was pretty nervous to say the least, and Jono was totally shitting himself.

We eventually made it to the hotel, but it wasn't really worth the wait; our room was tiny, with just enough room for a bed. This made Sarah cry even more.

The next morning, it was time to get skiing, and as me, Juppy and Sheena had never been before, we had to go to ski school. Afterwards, we were so knackered that instead of going up the mountain with the others, we headed back to the hotel and started drinking. I drank a lot, and found that I got on well with the receptionist – really well, in fact.

By the time the others got back, I was out of the receptionist's room and in my own.

The next day, we had ski school again in the morning, and then Juppy and I decided to go up the mountain with the others, so we got on the ski lift. Unfortunately, neither of us had ever been on this type of cable car before, and we didn't realise that you had to pull the bar down from above.

Jono was in the car in front of us and was waving frantically, trying to get our attention and to tell us to pull the bar, but as we were getting higher and higher, Juppy was hanging onto me, screaming and scratching me badly in his fear. Eventually, I realised what we had to do with the bar and pulled it down quickly – phew! We were probably pretty close to dropping to our deaths.

At the end of the ski lift, we didn't know how to get off, so we just stayed on, getting higher and higher until it started back down again. At this point, we jumped off, not realising it was around a fifteen foot drop to the ground. Luckily, we landed in soft snow, and so we managed not to break anything.

After the excitement of the ski lift, Juppy and I took it easy for the rest of the holiday, staying in the pub and the restaurant. One night, there were four or five lads sitting behind us as we ate, and I recognised them as being from the same hotel as us. They seemed a bit older than me and were typical Londoners: loud, rude and always trying it on with our girls.

They made a particular comment loud enough for me to hear (which I was sure was their intention) and that was it. I stood up and offered to take them outside. On hearing this, Jono started choking on a piece of bacon – he wasn't a hard man at all and neither was Juppy; they weren't used to confronting others.

As the lads stood up, eager to go outside and beat the shit out of me, the restaurant owner intervened, asking me to leave. I did, but my party stayed there to finish their meal. Now on my own, I found some other bars and got wasted.

All in all, it wasn't the best holiday ever. Sarah finished with me soon after.

At first, I was annoyed that I'd never had a blow job from her, but I was actually more upset than I thought

I'd be; I didn't take rejection well and I was in a bit of an emotional mess. This mainly manifested itself in me getting drunk – a lot.

Jono moved on yet again to a two bedroom flat in East Worthing, right near the sea, and I started flitting around between Carl Stabler's place and Dave and Riv's flat. The latter let me rent a room there, and it was a beautiful place. The location was ideal: right on the seafront. The window in my room even had a sea view – perfect.

After a while, Jono went off to Australia on a year's working visa, staying with Kev Packham, a Worthing boy who'd previously moved to Sydney. I said goodbye to Jono, promising him that I'd be out in a couple of months after I'd sorted my passport out.

I wasn't alone; my friends Darren and Tim – who'd just come back from America – wanted to join me in travelling to Australia in January, and it was them who helped me sort out my passport and visa. I got a brand new passport (so no more getting detained at airports due to my American deportation stamp) and got approved for a year's working visa, just like Jono. I was so excited, I couldn't wait to get out there.

It was early January 1988 when we went – although Tim and Darren flew out the day before me – and I had a very weird and interesting trip to Sydney. The plane's first stop was in Moscow for fuel, where we waited for a few hours. This was where I met a lady, and we talked for ages. She was beautiful, blonde and slim, although she did have a mole on her chin with hair growing out of it, which I thought was a bit weird, and which I couldn't stop looking at no matter how hard I tried.

On the next leg of the journey, we managed to get seats together in the smoking part of the plane, and we got on great, talking and laughing and passing the time. I got the sense that she wanted a bit, and I was proved right on our next stop.

This was in Naruto in Japan, where we had a few more hours to wait. We had a couple of drinks and then she went off for a shower (there were good facilities in the airport). When she came back, we went up to the observation deck to look at the planes coming and going, soon realising that we were the only ones there.

After a few moments, we started kissing, and when she pulled back, she looked at me and asked, "Would you like to fuck me?" I smiled. Yes, yes I would!

We found a secluded part of the deck, which was covered from the rest, and she pulled her tracksuit down to reveal hold-up stockings – so that's why she'd wanted a shower. What a dream start to my holiday; I rammed her hard and it was over before anyone might come round and notice us.

I took a few photos of her with my camera to show the lads when I got to Sydney – I knew they'd want evidence – and also got her address, just in case.

We went back into the airport for a few more drinks and then boarded our final flight to Sydney. On this stage of the flight, she put a blanket over me and snuggled. I thought it was nice, but I liked it even better when she manoeuvred herself so she could suck my cock. It was amazing, although it was made slightly more surreal by the fact that there were two lads about my age opposite, watching me. They clearly understood what was going on and I smiled at them knowingly.

She took the lot and then washed it down with a vodka and coke. What a flight!

When we finally got to our destination, I kissed her goodbye and off she went.

I had to wait several hours for my friends to turn up at the airport, and when they did, we headed straight for the nearest bar, having a few drinks and catching up about everything – including, of course, the woman from the flight. Afterwards, Jono took us back to the flat he was renting, this two bedroom place in a really good area of Sydney – it was a few floors up, overlooking the Sydney Harbour Bridge. This flat was owned by Kevin, who lived in the flat above, and while Tim and Darren stayed in the spare room, I got the fold out couch in the front room.

We crashed out, and the next morning Jono took us in his work van (which he'd got with his new building job that he'd had for a few weeks) to Tamarama Beach, where we stayed all day in the heat. Having just been in an English winter, the thirty degree temperature came as something as a shock, and we all got a bit burnt. Having exerted ourselves in the sun all day, we decided to stay in that night and have a few quiet beers in the flat.

The next day... wow. Tim walked into the room and I couldn't believe what he looked like – his eyes, mouth and nose were dwarfed by his head, which had become humongous overnight. He screamed, obviously in pain, which caused Darren to come running in. He looked pretty bad as well but nowhere near as bizarre as Tim – he looked like a freak in one of those weird, old-fashioned circuses. It took us all a while to realise what was going on, but it soon became apparent that he'd got heat stroke from the day before. Jono – who was fine, having lived in Sydney for a while longer – couldn't stop laughing; every time he looked at Tim, it would set him off again.

We did all the touristy things you usually do in Sydney, and before we knew it, it was January 26th – Australia Day. This year was the country's bicentennial: two hundred years since the first ships had arrived at Sydney, carrying the convicts. It's an important thing to celebrate, of course, but most people just use it as an excuse to drink and have fun, like any bank holiday in England.

We started at the Woolloomooloo, a pub near the jetty that Prince Charles and Lady Diana had arrived at. Needless to say, we drank heavily, and then we crashed in the botanical gardens for a couple of hours before heading over to The Rocks, an area of pubs and clubs. It was here that we witnessed the most amazing fight between scores of blokes who were going at it hammer and tongs, but we soon headed back down to the bridge and out of trouble. In this spot, we watched the most incredible firework display I'd ever seen, definitely something to remember.

After that, Tim and I stumbled up to the west end of the city looking for some brasses, and we soon came across a peep show. We went in and a girl immediately asked me to go with her upstairs, so I left Tim behind, happily watching the peep show on his own. When I got into the room with the girl, I must have flaked out pretty soon, as I woke up alone, with the door locked from the outside.

This was a problem, of course, but my main issue at that moment was that I really needed a piss. I was desperate, so I looked around for something I could go in, finding a basket with tissues in it. Well, they'd locked me in and not given me much choice, so I went in the basket. After I'd finished, the door opened and the girl walked in, shouting at me to leave and to take my mate with me, who was passed out, naked, on the peep show floor.

I was just leaving the room when the prostitute picked up the basket, screaming as the piss dribbled out of the holes like a watering can. I didn't stick around any longer – I hurriedly grabbed Tim and ran off back to the flat.

A few days after Australia Day, Tim and I hired a car and went up to the Blue Mountains, leaving Darren behind as he'd found a job already. On coming back from the mountains, I decided to try and find work over on the other side of Australia; I had a mate, Steve, who was playing football for a team in Perth, so I thought I'd go and meet up with him.

The lads took me to the coach station and I started on my three day trip. It was very hot, but comfortable enough on the coach, which had air conditioning and a toilet. We stopped every few hours to stretch our legs and we had one night at a travel lodge – a basic room but OK for a shower and for getting a bit of sleep.

We travelled through the Nullarbor desert, where the landscape was pretty much just miles and miles of sand, although I did see a few camels and a lot of kangaroos. We finally arrived in Perth around late morning, but I still had to get to Fremantle, which was a port city about fifteen miles away by train. It was actually really nice – very tidy and clean – and it had been spruced up not long before due to the America's Cup sailing regatta being held there.

Steve had told me he was working at Gino's Trattoria in the high street, which I found easily, and soon I was talking to my friend, who was serving coffee behind the counter. He told me he was the best coffee maker in Freo, and boy do those Italians like their coffee.

We had some lunch and then Steve took me back to his apartment, which he shared with two other guys. They told me I could stay there for a while, but that I needed a job to help with the rent. So, I started hunting, and soon after, I found some work through the local paper – they wanted ground workers in Bunbury, about 200 miles south of Fremantle.

Knowing I needed the cash, I rang the man who'd placed the ad and asked him if I could dig, to which he replied that I could. He also said that he was going to Bunbury the next day and that he could pick me up and give me a lift. This seemed perfect, so I agreed and quickly packed.

The boss man appeared in a big saloon car, along with three other guys, all Italian. Their English wasn't very good, as they'd only been in Australia for a few months, but I could understand them well enough. I understood enough to realise that I might actually die on this journey, anyway; the driver was an absolute maniac, singing and shouting back to the other Italians behind. The boss wasn't much help either – he was swigging wine and passing it around to the others.

Despite the potential dangers, we all got to Bunbury safely, where we were put in a trailer for workers. These consisted of a shower, a kitchen and beds, all in the same room – not what I'd been hoping for. Still, we were only going to be there for three weeks so I decided to suck it up, especially when they told us that if we dug the footings in less than the allotted time, we'd still get the full rate of pay for three weeks. Not a bad deal.

After the work had been explained to us, we had something to eat – which was brilliant; the Italian cook was fantastic – and then we went to bed. I didn't, however, get any sleep, not with all the farting and snorting going on around me. It was ridiculous.

Completely knackered, I started work the next morning, and found that it wasn't quite as easy as I thought it was going to be. For one thing, I hadn't worked for months, and my hands were suffering badly. I was given a weird, long shovel to dig with, one with no handle like something the Egyptians would have used, and my hands kept sliding down the shovel, blistering badly.

What we had to do was dig rows a metre deep and twenty metres long, then concrete them after each row had been completed. Our target was to complete six of these rows in the three weeks, although we all hoped to finish before that and leave early with our money.

It was hard work, not just because of my hands but because of the heat and the sun beating down on us every day; it was so fucking hot, and as it got up to 40 degrees some days, we had to start at 5 a.m. to try and beat it. It was exhausting, and every night after work, I'd shower, eat, and go to bed, with absolutely no energy left for doing anything else.

Still, the incentive was there, and we finished four days before the three weeks were up, still getting our full pay. I left as soon as I could and got back to Fremantle. I was knackered, but now I had enough money for me and Steve to rent an apartment at Mcatee Court. This was a really nice place, and we were able to use the shared pool and everything – a luxury I wasn't used to.

Thanks to my digging work, I could afford to stay there for at least a few months, and I had enough money to keep me going for a while.

When Tim came over from Sydney to visit for a few days, we hired a car and went up to Monkey Mia Dolphin Resort, where we swam with dolphins – an amazing experience. We also went to The Pinnacles in the desert and drank tins of Emu beer while listening to David Bowie tapes in the car. Great days!

Football also played a big part in our Australian adventure, for both me and Steve. He had come out to Australia in the first place answering an ad for young, good quality players, and was soon playing for Perth Italia in the West Australia League. He got on well there, becoming a main stay with the club. I used to go and watch them, and it was a very similar experience to watching football back in England; after the game, we'd all go out and have a ball.

After a while, Steve introduced me to a team in the lower division, Cockburn, and they gave me a trial for their reserves. I played well during the game, scoring two goals, and they agreed to take me on. I did well at Cockburn, but at the same time, another team in the top division let it be known that they wanted me too.

Cockburn's manager – Billy Thorburn – didn't want me to go, and he did everything he could think of to make me stay, even offering me work after the end of the season (which was in two weeks' time) if I stayed with Cockburn, and I agreed. The work was on an oil rig just off Perth, and I became a welder's mate for three weeks. This earned me quite a bit of money, and after much thinking, I decided that I'd go and visit Darren, who was now living in Ft Lauderdale, USA.

When I announced I was leaving, Cockburn threw me a going away party. The manager said that if I wanted to come back to Australia next season, he'd get me a sporting visa and I could play for the team, which was great – the thought of another season in Australia was really tempting.

Luckily, while I was in Perth, I got a visa for a short stay in America, despite my previous deportation from the country. My new passport helped, but if I'd tried it today – with the technology they have available now – I'd most certainly be declined. Steve easily sorted out a new flatmate, and I said goodbye to the girl below our apartment (whom I regularly shagged).

She took me to the airport and I got on a plane, ready for my next adventure.

Chapter Five

From Perth, I flew to Melbourne and then onto Hawaii, where I had a stopover for a few days. I got as much sightseeing in as I could and then went on to Ft Lauderdale, where Daz and Riv met me at the airport (Riv had come out for a holiday for a few weeks).

Darren took us back to his apartment – that he shared with his girlfriend – and then Riv and I hired a car, driving around for a couple of days before returning back to Darren's place.

He introduced us both to his boss, who was quite a character. He took us out on a hover boat, making me feel like I was in a James Bond movie or something, and then brought us back to his huge house – this guy was clearly doing OK for himself. We chilled out there, going in his hot pool and looking for alligators in the swamp at the bottom of his grounds. This was nothing like any of the places I'd stayed before.

One of the boss's friends, Manny, was introduced to us, and while he was a nice guy, he was also tough – he was a box fighter, someone who fought for money against any willing opponents. It was a seemingly strange thing for him to do; on meeting Manny, I imagined him to be anything but that. It was extremely brutal and most of the fighters he was up against were thick and took drugs – completely the opposite of Manny himself. I watched one of his fights, but one was enough for me, and I never went again.

I stayed in Ft Lauderdale for another couple of weeks before my thoughts started drifting towards home. After all, I needed to get some work back in England and start planning my trip back to Aus.

Daz took me to the airport and I set off for the UK – although this time, not in a mail plane. I got back to England in late October and went back to my room in Worthing, where I planned to stay until I left again for the other side of the world.

It wasn't long before Sarah, my old girlfriend, heard I was back and wanted to see me. So, she came over to the flat and we went out for a drink, where she told me she was living in Brighton with a bloke but that she was going to leave him because he was a bit of a gangster.

As I was made to believe that she'd soon be single, we went to bed a few times – obviously, the gangster wasn't treating her right and she needed a good session. Then, one night while I was having a bath, the phone rang. It was Sarah, and she was shouting that this bloke was going to find me and kill me. 'Fuck me,' I thought, 'I'd better get out!' And that's exactly what I did. I went over to Stib's house in Littlehampton to hide from the gangster, and luckily, I had to go down to Devon that weekend to play for Sussex in the national trophy, which helped me out a lot in terms of not being around to get beaten up.

Afterwards, I heard that Sarah's boyfriend did come over, and when he couldn't find me at my place, he stalked the Rhapsody bar, looking for me. It seemed that he thought Riv was me and was planning on 'giving him a slap'. He didn't do anything, however, and the whole thing calmed down again.

I kept out of Sarah's way after that – and I still didn't get that blow job!

That Christmas was heavy, with a lot of parties and a lot of drinking, and once the festive period was over, I got some work from Carl Stabler while I was waiting for my sports visa to come through from the passport office.

When it did, I couldn't wait to get going, and I hopped on the first plane to Australia. Unfortunately, the flight wasn't quite as eventful as my first one had been, but I was looking forward to landing back in Aus. We had one stopover in Singapore and then we went on to Perth.

Steve picked me up from the airport and took me back to his new apartment, where he'd saved a room for me. It was a nice place – a tidy flat right by the park near the Harbour.

As soon as I could, I started playing for Cockburn (the team who were sponsoring me) but it wasn't quite as good as I'd hoped – for one thing, they were skint, and they could barely pay me. Apparently, the manager thought I'd just be grateful to be sponsored, as it would mean I could spend another year in Australia, and while I was definitely grateful, I needed money; I couldn't live off nothing.

One week, a farmer – who was a supporter of the club – gave me 36 eggs, which made me laugh; I must have been the only professional footballer to get paid in eggs! My friend Ben from Leeds was over in Australia as well, playing for Athena, another division one side. He stayed with us for a while, and never once did he get paid in eggs. I couldn't even move to another club, either, due to the conditions of my sponsorship. I simply had to get some other work.

I did some washing up at Gino's, as well as some labouring work for a block paving company, but it wasn't for much money and I wasn't having fun there. The weekends were always good, though, and I started playing basketball for a team, but as I didn't have much money and was working in shitty jobs, I wanted to get out of Australia as soon as I could. The only problem with this, of course, was that I had to save enough to buy a ticket home (the club were meant to fly me home, but as they had no money, they couldn't). Getting desperate, I rang Riv to ask for help, and he – along with another good friend, Wakey – bought me a plane ticket back to England.

Soon, I was (yet again) on my way back home, and Riv came and picked me up from Heathrow in September.

Not wanting to waste any time, I immediately rang the chairman of Wick, who agreed to pay me £1,000 as a signing on fee. I agreed and straight away I paid back what I'd borrowed from Riv and Wakey, clearing my debt to both of them.

In the meantime, I went back to working with Stabler, and in 1990, I passed my driving test – about time! This was one of those intensive courses with a test at the end, so it didn't take up much time, and soon I was able to expand my job possibilities.

Riv worked for Dave's shop fitting company, Motif, who made exhibition displays for sports brands such as Fred Perry. I got work driving for them, going all over England and picking stuff up, and I even got to go to Germany and France, helping to put up the stalls at the exhibitions.

At an Expo in Munich, I got talking to a beautiful dancer from the Adidas stand while I helped move something for them, and soon we were both in my van out the back, where we had an hour of bliss.

I liked flying out to various cities with Motif, but unfortunately, the work wasn't constant, so I went back to work for Carl on the concrete. After a while, Dave's girlfriend and Riv's girlfriend both moved into the flat, so it was time for me to move on.

I got a room in a house in East Worthing, along with my friend Billy Elliot (whom I knew from football and the pub) and 'Fat Bloke' (the barman at Rhapsody's). Fat Bloke had just moved down from Horsham, although he thought of himself as a Londoner, 'The Pearly King of Horsham.' As well as bartending, he dabbled with decorating and plumbing, doing all sorts of odd jobs for people. It was a good household, and the three of us got on great.

That Christmas was pretty special. I decided to cook Christmas dinner for my friends, and there ended up being twenty-five of us. I went all out, putting up tables and decorations in the lounge and dining room, and borrowing glasses and plates from the pub. Paul and Dizzy helped me prepare the food, which was a 25 lb turkey and all the vegetables you could want, as well as stuffing, white sauce, cranberry sauce, and seemingly hundreds and hundreds of roast potatoes. It was a huge success; everyone loved the food and the house remained relatively undamaged. After the festive meal, we all went out on the town and had a really great night. It was definitely a Christmas to remember.

At that time, other aspects of my life were also going pretty well. I was soon to be thirty years old and I was still enjoying playing football, as well as having an active social life. I had been on good form with the ladies, and was more or less content with my lot.

Then, everything changed. One night, Billy brought a girl, Rachel, back to the house, whom we'd both met the week before. Billy – who was pissed – had told her to come back and see me, which was fine by me as I really liked her. Little did I know it then, but this girl was my future wife!

Rachel and I talked and talked and had a right laugh, before she got into my bed. We didn't do anything sexual, though, at least not that night – it took about two weeks before she succumbed to my charms.

She was six years younger than me, and I knew of her through her friends Debbie, Collette and Michelle, who used to come down the park and who cleaned our flat for a while. Rachel lived in a house in Worthing and she had a young daughter, Clo, who I got on well with. I used to go round their house all the time, where Rachel would always feed me – she was a great cook.

One day, she asked me round 'to talk' about something, and my first thoughts were that she was going to ask me to move in with her. So, I went over, completely expecting her to ask me that question, when instead she told me something else: she was pregnant.

Shocked, all I could say was, "Oh?" and then I left, needing to be on my own and to think everything through. I went for a walk, a million thoughts and feelings flying around my head. Did I really want this child? Did it even matter what I wanted? After all, I definitely wasn't going to ask her to get an abortion. After a while of deep thinking, I decided that this child was meant to be, so I went back to Rachel and told her that I was delighted, that I couldn't wait to have the baby with her, and that I would move with her and Clo into the new house she was going to get.

A few months later, I did move in with them, to a big house on the main road near the Worthing golf course. It had three bedrooms, a nice kitchen, and a front room – ideal for us. We got on fine and I made sure I worked hard in preparation for the baby. The closer it got to the end of the nine months, however, the more unsure about things I became, but I was just getting nervous, and when it got close to the birth time, I settled down. I was actually looking forward to it.

One morning at about 3 a.m., Rachel suddenly sat bolt upright in bed, saying that her water had broken. "Don't panic!" I said, even though I most certainly was. Trying to keep calm, I got Rach into the car and drove her to the hospital, where she was put straight into a delivery room. I stayed with her, although I wasn't a huge fan of all the grunting and groaning that was going on.

After a few hours, Rachel was ready to push, and I was asked by the nurses to look as the baby's head started to appear. I have to admit – it was a little weird, like an action man coming out of the eye of your penis… it looked very, very painful. She screamed and pushed and the head came out bit by bit, and then he slid out.

It wasn't, however, the magical moment we'd hoped for, as his head was black, and the umbilical cord was wrapped around his tiny neck. I didn't know what to think – I was trying not to think the worst – and in my panic, I wasn't doing a very good job of calming Rach down, either.

Well, an alarm rang and more people came running in, looking at the baby and talking fast. After a few seconds, one of them took him and held him upside down until the blood rushed back into his head, and after being checked over, he was given to me to hold. Phew!

It wasn't a nice thing to witness, but the pure relief that he was OK made everything else fade into insignificance. Rachel was fine (although still a little shaken, obviously) and she had to stay in the hospital for a few days.

After I'd made sure she was OK, I went home and then went for a drink or two – OK, loads – with the lads to celebrate.

A few days later, when Rachel and the baby were settled at home, we had a lot of visitors to welcome him into the family. Clo in particular bonded with the baby immediately, and it was great to see them together.

We called the baby Ryan, due to a bit of a tradition in my family. My dad's name was Robert, my name is Roderick, and my two brothers are Robert and Richard. I thought I'd carry on the R name tradition, so Ryan it was.

Those were the good days.

Chapter Six

Now for some more memories from my time playing football, of which there are many.

I played for Wick for nearly ten years, a decade during which I had a great time, made some brilliant mates and had some good support, from both friends and family. My dad even used to come to away games to see me play, meeting up with Tommy Stabler, Carl and Stibs' dad. They'd also hang around with Barry Wadsworth, the chairman, and Jack Croft, a director.

After the game (whether we won or lost), we'd go to a pub – preferably a country one – and have a real laugh. One game we played at these pubs was called 'Spoof', which involved coins. Basically, you had to guess how many coins someone had in their hand, between zero and three. So, say if there were five players, the maximum number of possible coins would be fifteen. The last two left in called it and whoever lost had to pay for the round. There was a bit of strategy involved and it sometimes used to get quite fractious, especially if there were a lot of people playing it.

I'd always have a good time in the pubs after the game, and thinking back now, I'd forgotten how many football clubs and pubs I used to take my clothes off in. In my early Wick days, my then-girlfriend Sarah used to come and pick me up so we could go out for the Saturday night, no matter what state I was in or how many of my friends were with me. The poor girl used to cram in four or five of my teammates into her little Renault!

I've mentioned that my dad sometimes came to my away games, and he also used to come for drinks with us – man, could he drink! He was always in his element at the pub, cracking jokes and telling stories while he got wasted with Tommy Stabler, Barry Wadsworth and Stibs.

One year, Wick went on an end of season tour to Jersey, and there were about thirty of us. My dad didn't attend this, however, as he had an artificial leg, and it was a bit of a nightmare when it got jammed rigid – I couldn't always cope with this, and the idea of it happening in Jersey when we were trying to have a good time didn't really appeal to me. The leg used to jam all the time, and occasionally I'd have to stick it out of a taxi's window in order to get him home.

Anyway, Barry, Tommy, Stibs, Carl and Jack all came along to Jersey, and we flew out of Southampton one Friday morning. The group wound up Marvin, the grounds man at Wick, by telling him they hoped he had his passport with him. As he wasn't the brightest, Marvin started to panic, and we told him the truth just minutes before he was about to go back to Wick. Cruel, yes, but it was just a few lads having a laugh.

Well, the tour started, and it was chaos. There were pubs and clubs everywhere, and we decided to visit as many as we could by hiring bikes and going on a mass cycle ride round the island, stopping at the pubs as and when we could. It was the usual stuff, and on Sunday morning I woke up with some Scottish girl. Looking over at the other side of the room, I saw Stibs in action with another girl, so a standard kind of weekend really.

We eventually managed to get back to the hotel and carry on drinking, and how we all got back to England safely I have no idea.

At Wick, we had the same squad for around five or six years, and I made a lot of good friends there: Welly, Crofty, Geoff, Wiz, and many more. We still keep in touch now. We had a lot of success, too. We won the County League in the 89-90 season, as well as the R.U.R cup and the League cup before winning the Sussex Senior Cup in the 92-93 season.

Norman Cairns was the manager for the whole of my career at Wick, and how he put up with me I will never know. Personally, I scored over 200 goals in 450 games, although I lost some games when I had two seasons in Australia.

I always had fun at training and when it was my turn to take part, I used to see who could kick the ball the highest, as well as having naked penalty shoot outs and playing British Bulldog, amongst others. It was a successful team and fun for all involved – I look back on those times with a smile on my face.

* * *

By this time, I was in my thirties, and now with a family to look after, I had to work hard at several jobs to keep the money coming in.

In 1993, I had some very sad news, as two of my friends died that year. The first was Andy Faggot, my gay Brighton friend, and the second was Mick Green, a football friend from Eastbourne. Both were really tragic deaths, accidents that were hard to picture or wrap your head around. Andy fell off a ladder while putting some posters up in a Brighton nightclub, and Mick got buried in a trench while he was laying drains. He was pulled out but he died a few days later – Rest In Peace to them both.

There was another tragedy that affected one of my friends too; Stibs' wife died from a brain haemorrhage, leaving him with Zenya, their one year old daughter. It was a tough year for everyone.

While Carl took time out of work to help his brother with the baby, I left concreting for a while and got a job – along with Sloggett – at the Tilbury Douglas construction company, building a bridge over the A24 just outside Worthing. When that job came to an end, we took up some work in Surrey for Nynex, the cable laying company.

Along with Grant, Rovik and Sloggett, I used to go up to Surrey to pick up a Nynex van and then put the trenches in the streets for the houses to be connected. We had to dig 30 – 40 metres' worth and then backfill it, ready for a Tarmac crew to re-Tarmac the pavements. First, a top cutter would come round and cut a channel off the Tarmac (30 – 40 metres long), and then we had to dig a depth to put the ducts in – the dig was deeper depending on the number of ducts we had to put in. We used to give the top cutter a drink to 'persuade' him to come to us first, enabling us to start earlier than the rest of the gangs.

It was hard work digging then filling in the ducts, and sometimes there were three in a trench, backfilling ready for the Tarmac gang. It didn't matter what the weather was; through rain and wind, we had to do everything we could to get our metres done. Luckily, we used to manage enough metres a week to get a good wage out of it, but we really did have to work hard for it. You couldn't cheat, either; every week, an inspector would come round all the trenches and put a probe down through them, measuring the depth of the top of the ducts.

After a while, we got moved to Worthing – where they were also getting Nynex – but this proved to be no good, as the area had predominantly slabbed pavements. This meant that we had to move the slabs in order to dig, and then relay them afterwards, which took up a hell of a lot of time. We were getting around 20 – 25 metres done a day and absolutely killing ourselves just to get that much completed. In the end, we decided it wasn't worth it, and asked for more money. They refused, so we left the job.

After that, I got some work with a guy called Martin Field, who was one of Sloggett's friends. I couldn't wait around for any other jobs to open up, as we'd just moved into a new home (the house we were previously in had to be given back to the Ministry of Transport, due to a new road being built). For the new place, Rachel made me get a mortgage, and I'm glad she did. I didn't know anything about that kind of thing, but I had a friend who was a financial adviser and who helped us through the whole process.

Incidentally, the house we moved out of is still there today and is privately owned – the road never went through.

In terms of our new house, I only saw it the day we moved in. Rach had seen it before, though, and I trusted her judgement. Anyway, she was going to be the one who would spend the most time there with the kids, while I was out all day working, and there was no need to worry – it was a nice house. It had three bedrooms and a bathroom upstairs, a kitchen and dining room downstairs, and a small but adequate back garden.

Our second child came along on the 2nd September 1997, just days after Princess Diana was killed. The birth was nowhere near as traumatic as the first one had been, and I decided to stop the tradition of the 'R' names, instead calling our new baby boy Frederick, which I thought was a cool name.

Martin (Sloggett's friend) was a builder by trade and when he got a contract for a company doing structural crack repair in Bayswater, London, he took me along with him. It was in an occupied hotel, where the top floor badly needed a lot of work doing on it. We both stayed in the hotel during the week and then headed home on weekends. A man called Tony was also staying at the hotel (the boss of an underpinning company), and the three of us hit it pretty hard in the bar most nights, sometimes going into town as well. It was fun, but I was always glad to get home to my family.

When the job in the hotel finished, I left Martin (he didn't mind) and went to work for Tony, underpinning in Tolworth, London. I used to leave my house in Worthing at 5.30 a.m. in order to beat the traffic, and while underpinning was probably harder than cable laying, I was fit enough for the job.

It was me, Tony, and Steve from Hailsham, and we used to have to go down inside a house footing that had subsided, around three metres deep. I used to fill two skips a day to get rid of the spoil, which was mainly earth and clay. We would then concrete the hole up to four inches below the existing bricks of the original house and dry pack the four inches with a screed type mix. It was incredibly hard work with long hours, and I used to be so tired driving home that I nearly fell asleep on numerous occasions. Slowly, the underpinning came to an end and I had to look for new work.

At around this time, my dad died in his sleep from heart failure. My mum – who usually slept in a different room to him – said that it was odd, as he'd said goodnight to her before heading to bed, something which was totally out of character for him. Perhaps he knew.

When she phoned me on that Sunday morning, I went round to the house to see for myself – yes, he was gone. While it was obviously a sad time, there were moments of comedy that could be found too. For instance, when the police arrived, my mum kept saying that while she hadn't killed him, she had wanted to loads of times. Then came the men from the mortuary. They went and retrieved my dad from his room, but while they were bringing him down to put him in the van, they dropped him on the stairs. I'm sure I could hear my dad laughing then – it's the kind of thing he would have found really amusing.

* * *

Not long after, a bloke rang me – Jon – saying he got my number from someone at football and that he might have a job for me, concreting a base for him in Steyning. As I needed the work, I agreed and went to meet him, where we negotiated a price. He was happy with how it turned out and said he had more jobs for me if I wanted them, starting with some damp proof work. As he had a lot of work going, and as he knew I had a good knowledge of South London, I agreed to work for him for a while, which was great for me as I needed the money.

Jon was an odd sort. A father of four, he was in his late fifties and was a Jehovah's Witness. This didn't bother me, but he never stopped trying to convert me, saying I could join the 100,000 people who were going to be saved. I would listen to him – neither agreeing nor disagreeing – and just let him go on and on about his religion.

His faith struck me as a little odd, as in general, he wasn't a very nice man. In fact, he could be violent and cruel, both to his nineteen year old son and to customers on his jobs. On more than one occasion, I had to stop him from physically attacking a client.

Still, it was money coming in, and he got a few extensions in both Worthing and London, which I continued to work on. It was pretty good at the time, as Jon wanted me to get all my tradesmen friends involved, meaning I could give work to my friends – after all, I knew plumbers, electricians, carpenters, plasterers... I even had Jono doing the brickwork.

By this point, I badly needed a break, and so I had a holiday in Menorca with the family and Rachel's mum to get away from it all. On my return, I finished a job in Shoreham for Jon, and during the work, he took the client round the corner – where no one could see them – and I heard Jon give him a slap over not paying. I didn't like how things were going and I was glad to leave, heading to Wandsworth in South London for the next job. I had fun there, having a laugh with two Newcastle lads who were decorating the inside of the house.

Jon would turn up most days to check everything was OK, but sometimes I wished he wouldn't. At this point, my friend Dabba was working for me. He was well into his twenties and fed up with his job, so he was heading back to university to get a sports degree. Before he went and changed his lifestyle, however, he'd agreed to do this work with me.

Anyway, Dabba was in the kitchen, and as he was kind of an easy target, Jon was being particularly nasty to him. However, one of the Geordies – Neal, who was covered in tattoos, some funny and some plain awful – was working in the kitchen too and overheard the bullying. Not liking what was going on, he shouted at Jon to leave Dabba alone. Bad move! Jon picked up a hammer, ready to attack, but Neal was just as quick, picking up a nail gun that had been lying on the floor just outside the kitchen. There was a stand-off for a few seconds, and then Jon seemed to realise that this tattooed Geordie wasn't fucking about, as he backed off.

Jon left, and that's the day I knew I had to get another job. Of course, I'd finish the current work, as the clients were smashing and I knew they could get me more work away from Jon the nutter.

The next day, I met someone else who would help me get more work – it's funny how these things happen. Basically, I helped a lady push her car up the road from the house we were working in, and as she was around my age and attractive, we got talking. Her name was Tabitha. As it turned out, she had some plans that had been drawn up for a gym in Earl's Court, and she asked me if I could have a look at them. I agreed, and the next day I went round, looking at the plans, which were for a gym and a juice bar, to go into a disused post sorting office.

It was great – it was my chance to get away from Jon and get going with some of my own work. I got on really well with Tabitha too, which helped, and the following Saturday, I went for a meal with her to talk about the job. I told her I could do it and immediately got onto Motif, the firm I used to work for. Mick – the boss – took a look at the plans and we agreed that with my men, his design capability, and his shop fitting guys, we could do it. By this point, I really needed to get away from Jon, so we quickly put a good quote together and sent it to Tabitha. I agreed to meet her one evening to discuss it, and we went for a drink while we talked about the money. As it turned out, she was far more interested in me than in the quote, and what can I say – I finalised the deal and got the job!

I couldn't believe it. I finally had my own work and I could get away from Jon – win win. We got told we could start on the work in November, so I finished the job in Wandsworth and informed Jon of my intentions. I told him I was going elsewhere (but with no more details than that) and left. I also told all my guys not to let him know about the job, and not to do any more work for him. No one needed to be dealing with that man if they could help it.

I felt fantastic. My first big contract! I had to stay in a hotel near to the gym site, but Rachel wasn't bothered – there was no love there anymore, and I later found out that she was actually enjoying not having me at home. Her new college friends were taking centre stage in her life, and there wasn't much room left for me.

Tabitha Ritchie (sister of Guy Ritchie, who had just married Madonna that December) had a big vision for the gym and juice bar. It was to be called Naked Health, and there would be a small gym area, dance and yoga studios, and studios for 'spinning' on stationary bikes (this American trend was brand new at the time). The juice bar was to the side of the gym so that passers-by could go in there and have a juice or a coffee without having to walk through the gym area.

The old sorting office needed a lot of work doing to get it looking like Mick's new plans that he'd drawn up with Tabitha, and it was going to cost quite a bit of money. I went up there before Christmas to have a look around and to get some things sorted, ready to strip it all out and get it ready for the renovation at the beginning of January.

After the Christmas period, we got the demolition team in straight away, as well as my plumber, Jon (not the nutty one), and Pete the roofer, who had a mile of repairing to do with Don, his Scouse labourer. While Pete wasn't on the roof, he and Don would help us inside, as there was a shit load to be done.

We stayed up for the first 4-5 weeks (in a three star hotel, which I chose, as I was essentially the boss) without going home, and I used to go out for meals with Tabitha in order to finalise all the details. She was a bit crazy, but generally a lovely woman, and she liked me a lot! She liked my team as well – we all got along well together.

Some evenings, Tabitha would take me to the Hurlingham Club in Richmond for swimming and dinner, and other evenings, I'd go with the lads to The Courtfield pub, or out for dinners in the West End. On these nights, Tabitha would always meet us in The Courtfield after work and go with us. She'd often get extremely drunk and I had to take her home on many occasions. The Courtfield was only ten yards from the back of the gym, which was good location-wise but was also pretty lethal!

The Motif guys joined us after a few weeks, but they were a bit older than us and didn't stay in our hotel. They also weren't big drinkers, which was lucky – if they had been, there wouldn't have been a hell of a lot of work going on. Some days, after a big session the night before, I'd be pretty useless, and I often walked over to the pub at lunchtime for some hair of the dog. Pete and Don would soon join me and sometimes we'd go on way past lunch. The job was going to take about four months, and it got to the point where I was looking forward to getting back at weekends and not actually having alcoholic drinks.

To start with, everything was going pretty well. The juice bar opened and the studios were taking shape – the spinning bikes turned up, and Tabitha and her team were busy drumming up business, getting members to join and publicising the soon-to-be-open gym.

Unfortunately, it soon became apparent that Tabitha was short of money. Quite a lot of money, in fact – about £150,000 in total. My bit was only about £8,000 but Mick at Motif was owed over £60,000. Tabitha didn't seem too worried, saying that her brother would lend her the money... but no. He didn't, and she was stuck.

With no more investment, the smart, trendy club was going to have to close its doors, a big blow for everyone involved. I got a phone call from Tabitha's partner, saying that I couldn't talk to her and that they were looking for investment. This broke me financially, and when the Daily Mirror heard about it and rang to ask if I would be interested in being interviewed, I didn't hesitate.

I actually had to go to the gym to meet the partners and the accounting team, and the Daily Mirror asked me if I would be taped for the meeting, to which I agreed. So, it was all arranged: that Thursday, I was going to go to a pub before the meeting, where I'd be introduced to the reporter (this wasn't at The Courtfield, by the way, it was in a pub further round the corner from the gym).

So, I met the reporter, who was a pretty woman around twenty-five years of age, and she brought me a beer while she had a wine. Then I had another beer and she had another wine… I think you can guess where this is going. We stopped drinking long enough for her to put the wires around me and under my jumper, and then we had a few more. We smooched in the corner of the pub for a while and then I realised I was late for the meeting. Not only was I late, of course, but I was drunk too.

The lady reporter walked me to the gym and checked my wired body before I knocked on the door, where I was greeted by a stern-looking gent. He could immediately tell I was drunk, and it really didn't help when I slumped down in a chair and the recorder and attached wires fell out from under my jumper.

I was quickly asked to leave, and I didn't mind – I wanted to go. I was just too pissed. Oh dear. Well, I went back to the pub and apologised to the reporter, who of course, was also drunk. We didn't have any taped conversations or anything… just some audio of me drunkenly gurgling. Oh well, such is life.

I never got any money from that job, and Naked Health was gone for good. Due to Tabitha's family, it was quite a high profile story at the time, and I was in the papers for a while due to the money owed me by Madonna's husband's sister, who had spectacularly failed to open her gym.

It was all new to me back then, but that wasn't the only time I've been put in the national papers…

Greece

Family and Mum and Dad

Alison, my first girlfriend

shine on you crazy diamond

Australia

THOMSON BAY
Rottnest Island
WESTERN AUSTRALIA

Me and Dabba World Cup

My young kids and Harry

The Committee before and after

Skiing, Italy

School

Roderick's record beating double

THE LOOK of determination says in the face of Roderick Wood (pictured right) says it all. For Wednesday was definitely his day.

He won four events at Chatsmore Catholic High School's sports day. He won the 100m in 2min 20.7sec, beating the existing record by 5sec. Roderick also won the 200m in 4min 44.6sec, beating that record by 15sec as well as winning both the triple and long jumps.

Other records went to M. McCready (2nd year boys) in 500m, and Kim Bealey (4th year girls) ran her 800m in 2min 58.5sec, beating the record by 15sec.

Teresa Abrels won the 2nd year girls 40m in a record of 7.2, topping 1.3sec off old record.

In the field, 13-year-old Vince Garzaro won the 2nd year boys long jump with 4m; breaking the record of 3.8m; Michael Jennings broke the discus record with 39.35m, a record 30.3m; and also the javelin.

Jenny Newbury broke the 2nd and 4th year girls 100m with 4.1/5m. (4.11m).

GIRLS

[small print partially illegible list of results]

BOYS

[small print partially illegible list of results]

RECORD-BREAKER Roderick Wood in action at Chatsmore School sports.

That old demon

DEMON TODD, the grease monkey Roderick Wood, disputes with a knife-blade razor, in a scene of Chatsmore High School, Worthing, Chatsmore production of Sweeney Todd the Barber.

Worthing Youth Team

Football

106

HAPPIER TIMES: Rod and Rachel Wood's marriage broke down after new claims but both now describe claims Carole Caplin was responsible

Cherie's guru did not finish our marriage

Daily Mail, Monday, June 21, 2004

Father-of-three is besotted with Cherie's style guru, say friends

Carole Caplin, her builder and the wife with a broken heart

TV show brings out the worst in contestants

QUESTION TIME: Rod Wood in the hot seat, right, and Jerry Springer, above

Builder's life stripped bare

CAPLIN HAS

KILLED MY MARRIAGE

That cow Carole is controlling Rod ..that's why we're getting divorce after 9 months

HAPPY...with Rod on their wedding day. (BELOW: Reuter today)

Recent

Chapter Seven

2001 was a tough year.

It started with the gym – the first big job that I'd got for myself had gone wrong. Even though it wasn't with the work but was with the payment, I still felt like a bit of a failure, as my first chance of earning good money and getting good contacts had failed miserably. I lost contact with Tabitha as well, who I'd liked despite the money issues, and who I probably would have gone out with if I wasn't already in a relationship.

Ah yes, my relationship. Things weren't good. I felt lonely and isolated, and in an attempt to try and bring the family together, I booked a holiday to Disney in Florida (all on credit cards). We set off to the States in June and had two weeks there, all of us sharing a large room in a Disney-themed hotel. Clo and Ryan were in bunk beds and Fred, the youngest, had his own single bed.

The kids were so excited, and I really bonded with them on that holiday, doing all the typical Disney things and going to all the parks. We also had a day at Sea World, it was great. Freddie wouldn't go on any of the rides, however, not even "It's a Small World." He'd just cry and have tantrums until we stopped trying to get him on anything anymore. He seemed happy, but he totally clung to me for the whole two weeks.

Rachel was the exact opposite; she was very distant for the whole holiday, and never kissed or embraced me, not even once. I could feel that she didn't really want to be there with me, which hurt, considering all the effort I'd put into organising the whole trip.

One day, there was an incident that I'll never forget. I'd gone off with Ryan somewhere, leaving Clo and Fred with Rach by one of the swimming pools. I came back just in time to witness Freddie getting hauled out of the water by a lifeguard – he was crying, but he was more or less OK. Rach came back with the ice creams then, screaming when she realised what had happened – that she'd left Fred asleep on the lounger, and that when she'd gone with Clo to get the lollies, he'd woken up and stumbled into the pool. That it can happen so fast is pretty unbelievable, but thankfully, all was good. Fred wasn't too impressed, though; he spent the rest of the holiday staying away from the water and saying, "No more glug glug!"

Eventually, the two weeks came to an end, and we headed back to England. We were all tired, but the kids had had a fantastic time, which is what mattered the most.

Of course, as soon as I got home, the same old feelings started to come back – I was alone and confused and didn't know what to do. I just wasn't sure what was going to happen to our relationship, and with the kids involved, that was a pretty scary thought. The arguments between Rach and I increased, and I decided that it would be a good idea to give us some distance and for me to spend some time at Jono's, where I could think.

Rachel agreed and so I moved in with him, going back to the house on the weekends to see the kids. During these weekends, Rachel would go off – to where, I had no idea. Things weren't getting any better between us.

It was a Saturday, the night before Fred's fourth birthday and the day England beat Germany 5-1 in Munich. I went round the house to watch the game with Ryan and to stay for the weekend as usual, but when I said, "Off you go then," to Rach, she stayed put. It was then that I realised she wasn't dressed or ready to go out anywhere. What was going on?

She asked me to go and wait for her in the front room, and once she'd got the kids sorted upstairs, she came in and sat down with me. Just as I couldn't believe what was going on in the football match, I also couldn't believe what Rach told me. Sitting up, she looked me straight in my eyes as she said: "I'm five months pregnant."

At this, I dropped to the floor in shock. Now, I've always thought of myself as being tough and not weak in stressful situations, and I don't often show my emotions or how I'm feeling, but sometimes, you have no control over how you react to things. I hope that I've installed in my kids that they should express themselves and be emotional. I don't want them to hide their feelings or bottle things up like I used to – I want them to be happy.

It wasn't that I didn't want another baby; the thought that was going around my mind at that particular moment in time was that Rach and I hadn't had sex since Christmas, which was over eight months ago. Thinking of this, I started crying as I asked her whose baby it was. She told me that it was a lad she'd met at college – he even used to babysit for us – but that he didn't want anything to do with her or the child.

I was in a daze. The game on the telly seemed as unrealistic as what Rachel was saying to me, and I was having a hard time wrapping my head around everything. I'd just come over to watch the football; I hadn't been expecting any of this!

My initial response was silence, and that's when I started to really think, to recollect all the times that my friends had said things to me, hinting that something had been going on with her and all her nights out. It was clear to me then exactly what she'd been doing during those evenings.

Something else occurred to me too: even though she said she hadn't known she was pregnant, she had stopped drinking and smoking weeks before, and she hadn't wanted to go on any of the rides in Florida. No wonder she was being so distant the whole time!

Well, of course, I was confused and angry, but I quietly and calmly asked her what she was going to do. Even though on some level I wanted to go and find this kid and give him a beating, I'm not a violent man and I knew that wouldn't help anyone or accomplish anything. In response to my question, she asked me if I wanted her to have an abortion. I couldn't believe it – how could I say anything to that? It wasn't fair. If she was going to do that, she would have done it, without bringing me into the equation at all. It wasn't my choice.

I couldn't stand being in that room any longer, and I went out for a walk, trying to think things through. I was completely emotionally drained, and feeling very low indeed. After a while, I went back to the house, where I lay down on the couch and tried to think – there was no way I could sleep.

The next day was Freddie's birthday, and even though I really didn't feel like it, I had to go to a local sports centre to set up his party in one of the hired rooms. This wasn't easy – especially when I found out Rachel had told some people about her pregnancy – but I just about got through the day, for Fred's sake.

I continued to stay at Jono's, keeping up the weekend arrangement with the kids, and Rachel kept asking me if I was going to come back to the house. It was tough, but after a lot of thought, I agreed and came home.

It was really difficult watching Rachel get bigger and bigger as she became more and more pregnant, but I decided that I was willing to take the baby on as my own. Clo and Ryan were OK with it, but I think it was harder for Clo. She was eleven years old at that point and was hurting, but she's a strong kid, and she got through it.

My prayers kept me strong and finally, the day came. I went to the delivery room to witness the birth, and little baby Harry was put straight onto my lap on the 11th of February. I cried again.

* * *

It wasn't easy, but as Harry got a bit older, I began to forget he wasn't mine, and we continued living like a happy family. I carried on working and, not even six months after giving birth, Rach got a job behind the bar at her mum's pub in Hove. This meant that she had to work evenings, and she didn't get home before midnight most nights.

By this point, I was nearly forty, and I was still doing some work in London. It occurred to me that having all the kids under my surname would make life a little easier, and so I asked Rach if we should get married. It wasn't a big, romantic proposal – it was more of a practical solution than anything – and I pictured the wedding being at the local registrar's office with just a few friends.

I should have known Rachel would want more. She needed the big show-stopping wedding, with a huge reception at Worthing Golf Course, bridesmaids, a Choccywoccydoodah cake, Cadillacs... the lot. It sounded like it was going to cost thousands, and it did!

My mind was all over the place, trying to work more than ever before to bring in money while simultaneously trying not to think about the wedding and how much it was going to cost.

I was recommended for a job in Brighton for a man called Tony – who had a couple of bars and a big gay club – and I arranged a meeting with Derek, who was going to be the project manager for the job, and who would therefore be in charge of my work. Luckily, I gave a good impression of myself and got the job, which couldn't have come along at a better time.

Derek was around fifty-eight, gay, and a really good artist. He was going to do all of the interior design as well as some artwork and murals for the interior walls – a big job. It was going to be a challenge, but I was well up for it – after all, how else was I going to finance this fucking fairy tale wedding?!

Talking of fairy tales, the job we were priced to build was going to be pretty spectacular, with stone balustrades around the first floor veranda, a huge, central, winding oak staircase, marble fireplaces and a big Victorian conservatory out the back of the house – it was going to be like a castle.

Excited about the project and the money it would bring in, I quickly got a quote together and took it over to Derek's to discuss it. He recommended me as a builder to Tony, but he asked for £400 a week in cash off me for guiding Tony's decision (that's what he said, anyway!)

Rachel was in full swing by this point, organising the extravagant wedding, and she even booked three nights in Rome for a honeymoon. Despite this, things weren't getting any better between us. The arguments were increasing and she was working more in the pub, getting home later and saying she was doing her bit towards paying for the wedding.

One thing that really put a dampener on the whole thing was that despite having a load of mates I could have asked, I didn't have a best man. This was because my friends – Jono, Sloggett, Jon, Paul... actually, all of them – didn't agree with me getting married, thinking that it was the wrong thing for me to do. I knew, deep down, that it wasn't right, but it had all gone too far by that point, and I couldn't back out.

So, in September 2003, we got married. The actual day went OK. We had over a hundred guests and Ryan (then aged eleven) was my best man – he did a great job. However, as the day progressed, I just kept thinking: What am I doing? *Why* am I doing this to myself?

Anyway, the Monday after the wedding we flew off to Rome, and we started the honeymoon as we meant to go on – by arguing, mostly. It was pretty bad. Rach just walked around the expensive shops, wanting stuff we couldn't afford, and we did the usual tourist things: the Colosseum, Trevi Fountain... all of that.

Then it went really wrong. We decided to go to a bar, where I drank far too much and wandered off on my own, leaving Rach talking to some guys. Well, my head was near enough exploding from thinking of all the wedding stuff and why I'd gone through with it, and I stumbled into an alley before stripping down to my boxers. I picked up a broom that was lying on the ground and started pretending I was 'The Spaniard' from *Gladiator*, which had just been released – a tremendous film!

Anyway, I'd just started attacking a lamp post when the local police got me down and carted me off. I spent the night in a cell and got released without charge early the next morning. Needless to say, Rach was not impressed.

When the honeymoon was over, we headed back home.

We were still arguing.

At this point, I was feeling quite low. What had I done?

* * *

For a few months after the wedding, at least, our relationship returned to what it was like before Rachel had announced her pregnancy with Harry, but then it started to go downhill again. I suppose it was inevitable, really.

Rachel started taking Ryan to rugby, which was a bit strange, as I'd never liked rugby – I wanted him to play football instead – and Rachel wasn't the sporty type at all. It seemed that she liked the guys there, especially the captain of the first team. Despite her lack of interest in fitness (she'd won a netball medal when she was ten, but apart from that, I'd only ever seen her run up the stairs), Rachel started playing touch rugby with the mixed adults, so I knew something was up. Then, one of my friends – whose son was on the Worthing rugby team – told me that Rach was getting very close with the captain I knew she liked. Very close indeed.

By this point, I was coming to understand that there was no hope for Rachel and I; our marriage was a sham and our whole relationship was pointless. She didn't love me. On realising this, I went to stay with my friend Dabba for one night, and ended up staying for eight years.

So, that was it. We decided to sell the house and both move on with our lives. As I'd recently put in a loft conversion, the house sold quickly, for £220,000. I got £30,000 and my clothes, and Rach got the rest and moved into a house in the town centre with the kids. She did pretty well out of the deal, it has to be said, and I used to wonder if she'd had it planned all along. My suggesting a divorce certainly didn't come as a shock to her – she immediately sat down and typed up the details: what she was getting, the rules and regulations, everything. She made it clear that I would be paying £450 a month for the kids' maintenance and clothes.

I used to see the kids most weekends, when I'd take them somewhere fun, like Alton Towers. I remember one trip there that was both funny and embarrassing. I went on one of the water slides, but halfway through my shorts flew off into the tunnel. The attendants had to stop the ride and I had to crawl out, naked, walking past the people who were eating their lunch in the restaurant. I suppose it was worth it, though; the kids found the whole thing hilarious and we all got a free meal out of it due to my less than sophisticated exit.

We also used to go to Fishers Farm Park near Horsham, which was an adventure playground with farm animals. It was a fun and safe place, and the kids could run around all day and play, stopping only to have their lunch. We went there all the time, no matter what the weather; come rain or shine – and even snow in the winter – we'd be there. We were there so much, in fact, that we became members, and sometimes we were near enough the only people there, such as when it was absolutely freezing. The kids loved it, though, so we braved the weather and always had fun.

One Saturday, however, everything changed. I went to pick up the kids as usual and they came out the house without Harry, saying he had a cold. I didn't think too much of it at the time, but the weekend after, it happened again. When I contacted Rachel, I wasn't allowed to talk to Harry on the phone either. I was trying to figure out what to do about the situation when a letter was put through my door (at Dabba's house, where I was still staying in one of his rooms). It was from Rachel, and it basically explained that she and her new boyfriend, Simon, were going to take responsibility for bringing Harry up. I was to have no say, as well as having no contact with him at all from that moment on.

I was furious. They couldn't do that to me! Harry wasn't a CD or a book I'd borrowed; he was my son. The letter went on to say that if I went round the house or threatened her or Simon, she would get the police involved. She said she'd already informed them of the whole situation.

This made me even more furious, and I stormed straight round there, knocking on the door and demanding to see Harry. No one answered, but the police turned up soon after, and while they agreed with my situation and my point of view, they said they couldn't do anything about it, advising me to go and see a solicitor. They confirmed that Rachel had pre-warned them about me, and that if I went round the house again, I might get arrested. I couldn't believe it, but I didn't have much choice, so I left the house without seeing Harry.

Those were horrible times, but I was still picking up Ryan and Fred every weekend (Clo was getting older by that point and was hanging out with her school friends, meaning it was just me and my two boys), and I was hoping that the situation would sort itself out, but sadly, it didn't. I haven't seen Harry since his fourth birthday, but I'm hoping he knows that it wasn't my fault. Luckily, Ryan, Fred and Clo used to tell him that I loved him, and that it was his mother preventing me from seeing him, and that I really did want to have contact with him.

Rachel asked if I would get a new birth certificate for Harry but I didn't – I've still got it in a drawer. One day I hope he'll come and see me, but I know that Rachel had her reasons, which I must respect.

During the ten years since Rachel and I broke up, I've been single, and I have absolutely no intention of being in another long-term relationship. Maybe as friends and the odd weekend away, but apart from that... no. I'm single till the day I die! (Again!)

Chapter Eight

My friend Peter was a journalist, and he knew many varied and interesting people. One of these people was Carole Caplin, the guru and fitness adviser to former Prime Minister Tony Blair and his wife, Cherie. Peter introduced me to her, and it was quite an experience to say the least!

So there I was, two days into a building job in North London, and I found myself lying naked on a bed with the weird smell of incense wafting up from downstairs, the scent mingling with the vanilla that was emanating from my battered, scratched and scolded body. The 'chanting' sounds of some tribal music from a CD in the bedroom was sending me to sleep, but I tried to keep my eyes open; I still had to drive my big, cumbersome van through the middle of London to the south coast and home, and it was already well after 9 p.m.

"Do you feel better now, darling?" she asked, her voice floating up from downstairs.

I shifted my body slightly, wincing at the pain. "Oh yes, marvellous!" I replied. I was lying.

The massage I'd been given actually felt like being beaten up, the bath I was ordered to get into was so hot you could have cooked a lobster in it, and the exfoliating cream used on my skin was like shards of broken glass.

It had all been exhausting, and I had been reduced to a state of fatigue, happy to be told to lie on this massive double bed, breathing deeply and relaxing.

"You'll be back on Monday with your electrician and plumber, Darling, won't you?" I could just about hear her voice over the noise of a smoothie maker, no doubt knocking up some sort of organic creation.

"Yes, that's right," I replied, wincing yet again as I pulled my boxer shorts up over my heat-swollen testicles.

I thought back to when she'd been bathing me. She'd said, "Now, stand up and I will exfoliate your body."

Considering I'd only met her the day before – when I'd been doing some renovation works to her flat and had happened to mention I had a little stiffness in my hips – I'd found this to be a little bizarre.

"I'm naked, though," I'd replied.

"Oh honey," she smiled, "you've got nothing I haven't seen or washed before."

Considering this, I stood up, the relief from the unbearably hot water being short-lived as it felt like my body – especially my genitals – was being sacrificed with what felt like acid, then rinsed off with freezing cold water. It was insane.

Later on, I slipped out the house, shouting, "See you Monday, Carole!" as I passed her, now upside down in her living room in some weird yoga position.

That was the beginning of the weirdest, most erotic, and most hilarious eight weeks of my life.

* * *

The next Monday, I returned to Carole's house early, this time with the electrician and the plumber. She lived in a swish place, and I had to press the intercom, go through the security gates, then punch in the entry code for the building before we could enter. Then it was a short ride in the lift up to the penthouse, from which there was a spectacular view of London. I was keen to show the electrician – who was an Arsenal fan – the ongoing building of Arsenal FC's new stadium, which was clearly visible from the flat.

Anyway, we alighted from the lift and I rang the doorbell to the flat while Gary the electrician and Jon the plumber talked excitedly about the woman of the house.

"Cracking bit of stuff, I've heard," said Gary.

Jon agreed. "Yeah, I heard she's got a real hot body and fabulous knockers."

We heard chains and locks being dismantled from behind the door, and a few seconds later, it swung open. "Hi guys," said Carole enthusiastically. "Marie will make you a tea or coffee if you want one. I just need to finish getting dressed then I'll be out of your way."

I smiled, and as I pushed Gary and Jon into the kitchen, I told them both to close their mouths, which were wide open. You see, there was something I'd forgotten to tell them – that in the mornings I'd been at the flat, Carole had walked around in a see-through, white cotton nightgown, her breasts clearly visible under the flimsy fabric. In fact, it was impossible not to stare at the rouge of her large nipples, or at the way the nightgown hugged her well-shaped bottom, clearly showing that there was no other underwear beneath.

Jon and Gary were clearly affected by this view that had been presented to them so early in the morning – their faces were a picture.

"Fuck me! Did you see those tits?" stammered Gary.

"See them? I nearly got one stuck in my eye!" replied Jon.

Marie – Carole's maid/assistant/personal bodyguard – came in then, making Jon and Gary tea (green tea with goat's milk, of course) while I went and knocked on Carole's bedroom door.

"Come in, Rod. How do your hips feel? Did you get those supplements like I suggested?"

I smiled at her. "They feel a bit better, and yeah I did. I think they might work." I was lying again; my hips were killing me and I'd forgotten the name of every single supplement she'd suggested as soon as she'd said it.

Carole was sitting on the floor, cross-legged, brushing her beautiful long, dark hair in front of her face. She didn't seem to care that her nightgown was nearly fully undone to the navel, allowing me to see practically everything. "I've got more things for you to do, Babe. There's the roof garden, the tiling, these doors... oh, loads." I nodded in agreement and she carried on. "I can't stop now, Babe, I've got a client at 8 a.m. then I'm doing a pilot for a TV show. Will you be here tonight?"

"Not tonight. I'm staying up tomorrow though in a bed and breakfast as I'll be working late, loading up the van with rubbish."

Carole, however, wasn't having any of this. "You don't have to stay in a B&B, Darling. I've got a spare room here doing nothing."

Blimey! I thought. Last week a bath and a massage, this week a sleepover! She was a lovely looking girl with a great body, and I started to wonder if I should go for it.

Why not? "Well," I said, "how do you fancy going to the pictures and having a bite to eat after?"

"That would be great," Carole hastily replied.

After that, I went and found Gary and Jon, telling them what needed to be done in the flat. Carol rushed past, saying "Bye bye!" in a theatrical fashion, and then I got on with some work, thinking how interesting the next evening was going to be.

* * *

As I drove up to London at 4.30 a.m. the next day, I was deep in thought, and a little apprehensive. I wasn't nervous about taking Carol out, though (I was ready, having brought with me a smart change of clothes), instead, my dilemma was whether I should drink or not. You see, by this point, I'd found out that I was allergic to alcohol.

When I drank, it brought me out in cuts and bruises, and sometimes I'd wake up in strange places with not a stitch of clothing on. Indeed, a few times I had both cuts and bruises and a lack of clothing, with just a vague memory of causing chaos.

I decided I wouldn't drink that night, and as it turned out, I wouldn't drink at all for the next four months.

Carole was easy to talk to, and by that I mean she was good at talking, so that wasn't an issue. My main problem that day was actually nothing to do with that evening, but instead to do with the carpenter I had coming to work at the flat.

His name was Jed and he was… unique. Let's just say that his social skills were non-existent, he could do with washing more, and the noises that sometimes came from his throat made it sound like he had three weeks left to live. He would have been better off working isolated in a field or something. Around fifty years old, he was a chauvinist Geordie bachelor with a strong regional accent and an even stronger odour. He drank ten pints a night and smoked eighty a day, and I was bringing him to a house where the female resident swanned around in next to nothing!

Luckily, Carole had gone to work extremely early that day, and we had to let ourselves into the flat with a key that had been left in reception. The day went smoothly, and the lads left around five. I was just tidying up as Carole breezed through the door, asking how it was going. She seemed pleased with the work but asked what the smell was – had I been smoking in there? Had I trodden in something? It seems that even though she hadn't actually met Jed, he'd left his mark in her flat.

In the basement of the apartments there was a gym, a sauna and a steam room, and Carole said I could use them to relax in before we went out. I then went to the spare room I was going to be sleeping in, upstairs in the split level flat. There was no door to the bedroom – just strips of beads and tassels, a bit like going through to the back of a corner shop – and the bed was amazing. It was huge, with a purple throw on it and six of the plumpest pillows I'd ever seen. There was a Jacuzzi bath in the corner next to shelves of all sorts of creams and powders, a TV, a hi fi, and stacks and stacks of books. It led onto the roof garden, with its 360 degree panoramic view of London, and there were some brand new Calvin Klein boxer shorts on the bed. It had everything I needed!

I wondered for a second how those boxer shorts would be coming off later – would they be kicked off as I yawned and wearily slid into this Turkish delight of a bed? Or would they be ripped off frantically while in a lustful grapple with the seductive Miss Caplin? To be honest, I wasn't too bothered either way as I was so tired, but of course, I'd be up for action if called upon.

"Shall we walk to the cinema?" I called out to Carole, who was in her room getting ready.

"No, I'll drive, Honey!" she called back. "I don't want to draw unneeded attention to us!"

The cinema was only 100 yards away from her flat, but who was I to argue? Carole came out of her bedroom then, and she looked gorgeous in a green jumpsuit and a big, sweeping, colourful coat, her hair flowing like a waterfall over the fake fur collar.

So, we started on our journey to the cinema, trying not to draw any 'unneeded attention' to us. This involved us arriving in Carole's four wheel drive jeep with the music on the car stereo so loud people thought we were a carnival float, and then proceeding to bump up half on the pavement and half on the road (which had double yellow lines painted on it), before getting out of the car. I wondered what she was like when she actually wanted to draw attention to herself!

We watched the Mel Gibson directed film which had just come out, sitting at the back and making small talk every now and then. We liked the film and we felt very comfortable with each other. I didn't know that being a health guru meant you could eat an unlimited amount of Maltesers though!

Once we'd left the cinema, it was too late to go for something to eat, so we decided to go back to the flat where we could talk and drink sparkling water, sitting on the long, luxurious sofa in the living room.

I quickly realised that Carole, while larger than life, was a lovely, warm person whom the press had given a hard time to. Anyway, that's what I worked out from the press cuttings I was shown; the truth was, me and my workmates knew very little about her before we started working for her.

By this time, I was very sleepy, and I told her I had to be up early. She agreed, saying she was ready for bed too. She showed me up to my room and I thanked her for letting me stay. I didn't make any sort of pass at her or even attempt to kiss her goodnight – on some level, I obviously wanted to save myself from the potential embarrassment that might have ensued, especially as I still had to work for her.

Once she'd gone back to her room, I got undressed and melted under the soft cotton duvet, quite happy how the evening had gone.

"You comfortable, Sweetheart?" she shouted up to me.

"Fine thanks!" I replied, nestling into the pillows.

"You sure there's nothing I could get you?"

"Don't think so!" I said in response, sure that her voice was getting closer and closer.

"Nothing at all, Babe?" She was extremely near now. "Not even a cuddle?"

That's when the beads and strips of tassels rustled and parted in the doorway, and sure enough, there was Carole, completely naked. What a body! It could have been a twenty year old standing there: perfect breasts, curvaceous hips, a trim waist, smooth, lithe legs, and the pubic hair... well, it would have won best in show at any hedge trimming contest at Kew Gardens!

I instantly pulled back the quilt to let her get into the bed and her eyes widened as she caught a glimpse of my manhood. Like me, it was extremely pleased to see her!

* * *

A few hours later, I awoke in the half light of the morning. Not wanting to get out of bed but knowing I had to, I slowly slipped out from under the covers and quietly got dressed, trying not to wake Carole. It didn't work.

"You're not going already, are you, Rod?" she asked, sounding a bit perturbed.

I nodded as I continued getting dressed. "I gotta get back to Worthing to empty the van and pick the material up. Which means I have to leave…" I looked at my watch. "Now. Sorry."

Carole didn't seem too happy that I was leaving her lying in bed, but I couldn't help the situation. Anyway, I bet the last bloke who stayed the night with Carole didn't have a twenty year old van filled up with shit, a dodgy starter motor and half an exhaust that had to be nudged gently back to the south coast! So, I said goodbye and Carole sulked, moaning about how I couldn't just up and leave like that in the middle of the night!

I drove back, extremely tired but with a wry smile on my face, thinking about the antics we'd got up to in the large, comfortable bed not too long before. Nice.

Around this time, I was working on the flat job plus another job in Euston (which wasn't far away), and I split my time between the two for several weeks, going back and forth. Mags and Slogs – who both worked with me – found it highly amusing that I would go back to

Carole's nearly every night instead of staying in the B&B with them. What could I say? I mean, I'd given up drink by this point, and a choice between listening to snoring all night or sleeping like a baby in a ten foot square bed with a beautiful, horny woman next to me wasn't much of a choice at all; it would be Carole every time.

She let me and my work mates join the gym she worked from and also asked me and Mags to help her with some modelling for her new book. We, of course, were happy to oblige, and I agreed to a photo shoot in the famous Harley Street. I picked Carole up in my van and took her to the clinic, where I was photographed while being treated by this top London physio. After the photo shoot I took her home, and she didn't seem at all bothered by the quite dirty mode of transport.

On the way back, Carole asked me what vegetables I liked so she could get some for dinner, and I was happier at this request than I perhaps should have been. You see, I was usually starving whenever I went round to Carole's flat; all she ever had in were organic things that looked like weird specimens in some lab, as well as perhaps some fruit and a little bread. I mean, the fruit was OK but it didn't really fill me up, so the prospect of some culinary delight was mouth-watering, especially as I'd lost a fair bit of weight over the couple of weeks I'd been with Carole – this was partly due to malnutrition and partly due to performing like an acrobat in the bedroom.

"I love asparagus," I told her, thinking of a lovely plate filled with meat and vegetables.

"Asparagus it is then!" she answered.

I dropped her off and then went back to work at the Euston job, thinking of the fine roast with all the trimmings that I'd be settling down to in a few hours' time. After work, I went back to her flat, where I used the gym and the sauna before coming back up, ready for my dinner.

"Eat it all up, Babe!" said Carole, smiling and placing a massive plate in front of me. Unfortunately, it wasn't quite the big roast dinner I'd been expecting; all that was on the plate were three different sorts of asparagus and a tiny bowl of organic dip. "Enjoy!"

Where was the meat? Where were the potatoes? Where was the gravy that I usually drowned all of my food in? Disappointed but not wanting to hurt her feelings, I tried to eat the plateful, but you can only eat so much of the stuff! Instead, I hid some in a vase, hoping she wouldn't find it later on.

Asparagus might be an aphrodisiac, but all it did to me was turn my piss greener than grass for about a month! Although, to be fair, we didn't really need any aphrodisiacs, not with the kind of stuff we were getting up to on a regular basis.

One night, Carole turned to me and said, "Tell me what you want me to dress in, Baby." Boy, what fun! Carole had the most fabulous wardrobe I'd ever seen, and that night I chose for her some thigh high boots, a leather mini skirt, a black, lacy thong and a matching top. I still get sweaty just thinking about it!

We had a lot of crazy nights, and I'm sure Carole thought that in certain positions during sex, I was moaning incredulously with pleasure, when in fact I was in a hell of a lot of pain – my hips were cracking and grinding, causing me great discomfort. I'd wince the whole time, but I wouldn't stop until the mission was accomplished. Some days, I had to practically crawl out of the flat, passing the reception area where the porter would look at me strangely – he must have thought I'd been playing British Bulldog all night.

Carole's phone was always ringing, no matter what time it was, and one evening it rang while she had hold of my 'old fella'. She answered the call with her other hand and started talking to Cherie Blair, who wanted some advice on what hat to wear when she met the Nigerian Ambassador (or something like that). Remaining calm and professional, Carole advised her, said goodbye, then carried on where she hadn't actually left off!

Not long after, my work was coming to an end at both of the London jobs, and I suggested we go away for a weekend. Carole agreed and we decided on Ibiza, as I had a friend there who could rent us his posh villa.

Not wanting to waste any time, I quickly bought two flights for the following weekend, and they weren't cheap. Anyway, I told Carole that I'd got the tickets and I was about to ask her for the £250 that her ticket had cost when she smiled and quickly said, "Oh, thanks. You're so kind."

Fuck! I needed that money, but I couldn't exactly ask for it after that without looking like an idiot, so I let it be. As it turned out, we never actually went, as someone out on the island had heard Carole would be there, and she didn't want all the media attention.

Speaking of media attention, it wasn't long after this that I was forced into the spotlight again, thanks to my ex-partner. She broke a story to the papers about Carole and me and how she'd apparently ruined our marriage – what absolute rubbish! I'd left home well before my first night in Carole's bed, and I'd left for very good reasons too. I couldn't believe it.

Well, Carole didn't want to be seen as a woman who had split up a marriage – even though she wasn't that person anyway – and so she thought it would be better if I no longer went round her flat. I understood her reasoning, but it was a bit weird – after all, I had nothing to hide. Plus, it was Carole who had first got into bed with me, not the other way around! So that was the end of that.

We still speak on the phone occasionally, and I still think she's a great person. More than anything, though, I have many great memories of that late spring/early summer of 2004.

Chapter Nine

I still had some tickets to Ibiza, and as Carole and I were no longer together, I decided to go by myself. What the hell! I thought. I was single and I seriously needed to get away after everything that had happened, even if it was just for a couple of days. I was still messed up about the whole thing with Rachel and Harry, and I'd stopped drinking for a while, which was how I usually coped with things. So, Ibiza seemed like the perfect remedy.

It also helped that my friend Julian lived out there, and had been there for over twenty years. He owned a little apartment and a couple of bars in the main town, and he knew the island inside out. He was nice enough to pick me up from the airport and take me back to his place – he only ever let friends and family stay there, and I was going to be the only one living there for three nights.

As soon as I got there I had a drink, something which I most definitely needed after the madness of the past few months. The alcohol was heavenly, and I'd soon had another one, then another one, then another one. I'd arrived in the evening and I continued to drink with Julian at his bar until the early hours.

I also carried on the next day, when I started drinking after breakfast. It was great; I lay by the apartment pool and just forgot about all of the shit that had happened over the past year or so.

I soon got talking to a couple of lads from London who were staying in the apartment next to mine, and when Julian appeared to see if I was OK and to tell me he'd put my name on the guest list for one of the top clubs in Ibiza, I asked if he could add my two new friends as well. He said it was fine and I couldn't wait to go; the two lads had been to that club before and it sounded amazing.

I decided I should probably stop drinking for a few hours in order to start again in the evening, and the lads (who were around twenty-five or twenty-six) said they had something that would keep me awake, no problem. Even though I hadn't had any drugs for about fifteen years, I figured I was on holiday so what the hell!

I had a bit of a kip then got showered and dressed before heading over to the lads' apartment. It was great, like I was going back to my early hedonistic youth, and although I'd never taken ecstasy before, I popped two straight away and followed them up with line after line of cocaine.

I vaguely remember dancing naked in a cage in the club – probably the oldest cage dancer they'd ever seen – and I just had such a great time. It was a brilliant night and exactly what the doctor ordered.

I was still going strong the next day, popping an E for breakfast and drinking and dancing until I collapsed back at the apartment pool, where I slept on a sun lounger until morning. It was my last day, and Julian gave me a few hours to sleep it off before he picked me up and took me to the airport. It was a manic couple of days and my head was completely frazzled, but in a good way.

When I got back to England, I went straight home to my room at Dabba's and crashed. It took me a good few days to recover.

* * *

This trip reminded me of another one I took a year or two previously. It was the first stag party I went to abroad, but I didn't really fancy it – it was for Rachel's brother Simon, and I only knew about eight or nine of the thirty blokes who were going. At this point in time, my relationship with Rachel wasn't great; she'd started going out in the evenings, practically forcing me to go out too, presumably so she'd be free to do whatever it was she was up to. Things weren't going well between us.

Her brother Simon was a few years younger than me, and despite the fact that he was a Tottenham supporter, I liked him. So, I agreed to go and I met up with the party at the Southdown pub, which was Simon's local. The drink was flowing but we soon had to leave to get the coach to Luton, where we'd be spending the night before flying off to Barcelona the next morning. I must admit, it was a right laugh in the hotel; Robert (Rachel's other, younger brother) was on top form, being very drunk and therefore very entertaining.

As I knew how heavy the next couple of days would be, I went to bed a few hours earlier than the rest, all of whom were carrying on with the drinking session. I'm glad I did, as the next morning I felt fine, while Robert had to be helped out of bed after having crawled into bed just an hour earlier. He looked like shit.

Anyway, we just about managed to get to the airport, where, of course, we carried on drinking, and soon we were in Barcelona, meeting up with Julian, who had come over from Ibiza and who was Simon's best man (they'd been friends since school). It was so much easier having Julian there, as he was fluent in Spanish, unlike the rest of us.

We got on a coach to our hotel, and after checking in, we went for a stroll around the city, just taking it easy, sitting outside cafés and having a few beers. Then we returned to the hotel, had showers, and got ready to head to Camp Nou, as Julian had sourced tickets for all of us to watch Barcelona play in the league. It was a great game: Barcelona won 4-0 and I watched Patrick Kluivert score a hat trick. We went back to the hotel after that, having a few beers before crashing – we were all knackered.

The next day started in a similar way, as we went to the harbour and walked about in the sun, having a few beers to cool us down in the heat and relaxing on the beach – bliss. That evening, however, was a little different. Julian had organised a trip to a brothel for anyone who wanted to go, so after a nice meal at a nice restaurant, around half of us got in taxis and headed over to Madam Bang Bangs, which was a top class brothel. Julian had been there several times to entertain business clients of his, and we all trusted his recommendation.

The taxis soon pulled up outside a large, old house in the back part of the city, and after Julian spoke to a big man at the entrance, the doors opened and we were allowed in.

All I could think was: Wow! The house was absolutely huge and as we entered the main foyer, I could see at least thirty beautiful ladies – of all nationalities – walking around in the sexiest underwear I'd ever seen. It was Heaven, and I felt like James Bond, being surrounded by all these gorgeous women.

I went straight to the bar, and immediately this long-legged blonde started chatting to me while she rubbed my cock. Well, that was it – she walked me over to the cloakroom and the girl working there passed her a towel and a key. I had to pay about £60 and then she took me up this beautiful, winding staircase and into a room, where she proceeded to lie me down on this huge bed, undressing me slowly. We had sex and I was in dream land.

After we'd finished, I headed back downstairs, had a drink, then took two Japanese stunners up the stairs. Perfect. After that, I went back downstairs yet again, where I had another drink and chatted to Robert for a bit, who seemed to be enjoying himself. I took a black girl up the stairs, which was amazing, and then for my last visit upstairs (with a stunning Thai girl), I had to borrow some money off Julian.

We left in the early hours, totally skint but completely buzzing. What a night!

I had a smile on my face all the way to the airport.

* * *

The next stag do I went to abroad was in Prague, and it was for my old mate Phil Bonetti, who was getting married for a second time. I used to play football with most of the group who were going, and I knew them all well. They were generally about ten years older than me, but that didn't matter.

We all met up at the Thomas A Becket pub on a Friday morning, having a few drinks, a catch up and a laugh before getting on the coach to Gatwick airport. Naturally, we carried on drinking at the bar, and we even had a little singsong, which led to us being told to 'quieten down' before we boarded the plane.

It was evening by the time we arrived at the hotel in Prague, and on the way in I noticed this beautiful, long-haired girl standing outside. She was quite clearly a prostitute, and I wanted to ask her if she actually was one, but we went off for a meal and then onto a nightclub. By the time we'd staggered back to the hotel, the girl was gone.

The next morning, even though we were a little worse for wear, we got picked up by a coach and taken to a camp in a forest just outside Prague, where we played paintball. It was good fun. We split into two teams and spent the day firing at each other with these powerful paintball guns. Those bullets hurt, and I had the welts for days afterwards to prove it.

We had a few drinks in the canteen then returned to the hotel, where I noticed the same woman from the night before, standing in the same place outside the building. She just had to be a prostitute. Well, I started chatting to her and asked if she'd like to go for a meal with me, which she said she'd be happy to do. Before we went anywhere, I agreed with her how much it would cost for the evening and then for the sex after the meal, but I didn't let the rest of the lads know what I was up to.

I met her outside the hotel at 9 p.m. and she looked absolutely stunning; in her long coat and six inch heels, she seemed incredibly classy. In perfect English, she told me that she was thirty years old and that she was a gypsy, and then we went out for the meal. She was great company and very funny, and I was having a grand old time. After we ate, she took me to a bar that gypsies frequented, and it was buzzing. I danced and drank vodka and had a great time, not thinking that I could have been mugged or anything like that; strangely, I felt safe with this woman.

We left the bar in the early hours and went back to the hotel for the next part of the deal, creeping into my hotel room that I was sharing with a guy called Chunky. He was asleep in the other bed, so I started undressing her. What a body! When we actually started having sex, I looked over at my roommate and could see Chunky watching us with one eye open.

When I woke in the morning, she was gone. So was my phone. Shit! She did leave me a nice little note, saying how much she'd enjoyed the evening, but that didn't change the fact that she'd stolen my fucking phone! Of course, Chunky found the whole thing hilarious.

Our flight wasn't until lunchtime, so we had breakfast and went to the airport, where we had a few hours to kill. And what do you do at the airport when you've got a few hours to kill? That's right – head to the bar. I drank far too much far too quickly, and after a while, I could barely stand up. My hips were in a bad condition then, so when I'd had a few drinks, I just couldn't walk properly, which was annoying to say the least. Anyway, the lads managed to get someone to help and Chunky managed to get a wheelchair off one of the airport officials so I could get taken to the gate. Chunky told the official that I had a medical condition... well, I suppose I did, but the seven strong beers at lunch certainly didn't help.

With the aid of my friends, I managed to get on the plane and fly back to England safely.

* * *

I've lived a fair few places in my life, with family, friends and girlfriends, but I have great memories of living with Dabba, as it was so easy and relaxed, with no drama. At that point, I still had Ryan and Freddie most weekends, though not Harry or Clo, as she was older and hanging out with her friends instead.

Work was a bit hit or miss, as although I'd had a lot of jobs in London, I'd lost some of them after what my wife had put in the paper about me and Carole. I was quite low for a while, but I eventually managed to get a nice job in Esher, so it wasn't too bad.

In the summer of 2006, I went with Dabba to Stuttgart in Germany for the World Cup, and I had a great time. We flew out on the Sunday morning to get there for the five o'clock kick off of the England v. Ecuador game. Even though we didn't have tickets, I wanted to be there for the atmosphere, which was just amazing. All the fans were buzzing, the level of anticipation high, with everyone in a good mood. Well, they wouldn't be if England lost, but I was trying not to think about that possibility.

We met a guy called Jack Pearce at a bar near the stadium – he was the chairman of Bognor Regis FC, an FA official and a good friend – and we had a few drinks with him while I looked out for any possible ticket sales. Luckily, I managed to get one from a tout who was in the same bar as us – not cheap, but it was my first World Cup and it was well worth the money.

It was a beautiful day; the sun was shining, we drank plenty of German beer, ate a load of sausages, and to top it all off, we won! After the game, we headed back to the city and partied until it was time to go to the airport, where we got the last flight back to Gatwick, where Dabba's girlfriend picked us up. What a great day.

At this point in my life, I was in a bit of a quandary. I needed more than football and work, but I had no intention of getting into a serious relationship again. I did, of course, want a bit of sex now and again, but I didn't know how to go about this – I wasn't going in pubs and clubs then, so I had to take a different approach to meeting women.

Dabba suggested I should look on the internet, which I was a bit dubious about; I didn't want to join a normal dating website, as I didn't want a relationship. After a while of surfing the net, however, I found something very interesting. There was a site where you could meet professional women aged between thirty-five and forty, who were either divorced or single and who just wanted meals, drinks and sex, with no strings attached. Perfect! Liking the sound of it, I joined straight away and put a profile of myself up on the site. I said I was searching for a professional woman who was looking for a night out – perhaps a meal and drinks or a trip to the cinema – and hopefully, sex.

I posted it and quickly got contacted by a lady from Brighton who liked the look of me. I liked the look of her too, and we chatted and texted for a week or so before deciding to meet up. She asked me over for a drink and a bite to eat, and I went over that Saturday night. I was quite relaxed on the drive over, as I was pretty sure that sex was on the agenda, and if it was, I was ready: I had a couple of Viagra on me, thanks to my brother's supply.

I knocked on the door, now a little nervous, and breathed a sigh of relief when she opened the door. I'd been warned that some ladies used old photos of themselves on their profiles and therefore looked quite different in the flesh, but this woman looked exactly like her profile picture.

Smiling, she ushered me into the front room and poured me a drink. I only had the one in case I needed to make a quick getaway, and I popped a Viagra in my mouth when I went to the bathroom. When I came out, she was already undressed, revealing some very nice stockings and suspenders. She was looking straight at me, her massive, false tits clearly on display. This lady obviously knew what she wanted and she got it all night. The next morning, I got up early and drove home, thinking, yes! This was what I was looking for.

The next woman to contact me was a divorced doctor from Suffolk, the same age as me. Even though she lived a little further away than I would have liked, she looked stunning, and I just had to give her a chance; I knew that I'd end up kicking myself if I let her go. We started talking and after a while I arranged to meet her for coffee at the Bluewater shopping complex by the Dartford tunnel, as it was about half way between the two of us.

She was exactly as I expected – classy and lovely. We had coffee and a good chat and then arranged that I would drive to her home in Suffolk the following week. On second thoughts, I quite liked the idea of the drive and the distance apart. So, early on a weekday morning, I left to go to Suffolk with another two Viagra with me for backup. It was a three hour drive, but I eventually got there and found her little cottage along a little country lane. She'd obviously heard the approach of my car, as she was standing outside the front door, already in sexy lingerie. What a greeting!

She didn't hang about; she clearly needed it quite badly, and she took me straight up to her bedroom. With the two Viagra working for me, we had a couple of hours of absolutely blinding sex. I even took a few pictures on my phone and sent them to the lads on the job I was currently on – they liked seeing pics of my outings. I drove back to Sussex then, tired but smiling.

I went to Suffolk a few more times until she started dating, but I still keep in contact with her today.

Chapter Ten

I'd got to the point where I wanted more out of life. Even though I loved building, and even though I'd figured out how to meet women who wanted no strings attached, I needed something else, something different.

I told this to my journalist friend Peter and he told me to join Star Now, a modelling, acting and extras website. He even set up a shoot with a professional photographer so I could get some decent profile photos. This was with his friend Helen, who lived in Surrey and who made me a portfolio, as well as introducing me to a few more agencies that would take me on their books. She was a lovely woman and I made sure I repaid her for all her help – I did some work round her flat and we occasionally had sex. So, once I'd got my photos, I joined Star Now and some other agencies, ready for whatever was waiting for me. Recently, I've also been taken on by Ray Knight, the best supporting artists' agency in London, which is great.

I'm particularly glad that I joined Star Now, as Peter had suggested, as through that I managed to win £10,000 on a game show! It was called *Nothing But The Truth* and it was presented by American talk show host Jerry Springer on Sky One. I had a pretty good guess as to what kind of show it was from its name, and I went for an audition in London. Luckily, they liked me, and I was asked to go for a lie detector test the next week, where I was asked a load of questions, mostly about me and my life.

For the actual show, there was to be a panel of my family and friends, and they'd be called up and asked questions before my liar test. The questions were pretty raunchy and revealing, but hey, what do you expect? It was a Jerry Springer show after all.

I was told I'd be called up for the show the week after, and the following Friday, me and my panellists were all picked up in a big car and taken to the studios in Hammersmith. The people on my panel were my mum, Dabba, Jono, and his wife, Jenny.

When we got to the studio, I was taken off and put in a room by myself, after which I was made up and given a plain T-shirt to wear. I was pretty nervous by then (the show was being filmed in front of a full studio audience of three hundred people) but I couldn't do much about it at that point! Soon a woman knocked on the door, sticking her head in and telling me that I'd be on stage in ten minutes.

The show involved the asking of more questions, and for every question I answered correctly, I would receive £1,000. However, if I then got a question wrong, that was it – I'd be out, without a penny.

With this in mind, I walked out onto the stage, looking at my panel at the side of the set. Most of them were sitting there giggling, apart from Jono, who just looked like he was about to shit himself.

Jerry introduced me to the audience and then chatted to me for a while as I sat in a big armchair at the front of the stage. The people in the crowd were good, cheering and whistling, and Jerry was perfect, just right for this type of show.

We started the quiz and I answered correctly, finally getting up to £10,000 – a good sum. The questions were pretty much as you'd expect; there was one asking if I was in the 'mile high club', and another asking if I'd ever had a 'back, sack and crack'. My mum was a bit oblivious to most of it but she did say some funny things to Jerry.

By the time I got to £10,000, I thought it would be too risky to continue, so I said thanks to Jerry and bailed out, ten grand richer! As it turned out, the next question would have been, "Would I like to sleep with my best friend's wife?" I had answered this before and had said yes – if she wasn't married. That was not a lie.

With that, I got off the chair and left. Woohoo! What a great buzz.

* * *

As I've mentioned, by the time I'd got to my forties, I was really trying to live my life and wanted to try out all sorts of different things. Even though I still had the kids on a regular basis, Ryan and Freddie were older by now and doing their own thing, which left me with more time to try something new.

As I was contemplating this, Dabba asked me if I'd like to go on holiday with him, his girlfriend Emma, his married friends Sean and Kerry, and their friend Nathan. They were planning a snowboard break to Nevada in the USA, and as Emma worked for Virgin airlines, we managed to get a real good deal on the week's holiday. I was excited to go; even though my hips were really bad and I knew I'd need them replacing,

I was happy to experience the snow and the beautiful scenery.

We left just before Christmas in 2006, flying to San Francisco before hiring a big hatchback car to drive to Lake Tahoe. It was a seven hour drive, and Nathan and I had to squeeze into the two jump seats in the back.

We finally got there, checking into the hotel at about 11 p.m., where I was sharing a room with Nathan. I didn't feel like going to bed though, so I wandered down to the casino and spent a few hours playing the tables. The next morning, Emma and I had to attend snowboard school, as neither of us had ever done it before, and I found it incredibly painful because of my hips. As it turned out, on our first trip up the mountain, Emma fell over and broke her wrist, so I stayed with her for the rest of the week, neither of us wanting to do any more snowboarding.

We'd go up the mountain by cable car then spend all afternoon in a beautiful café/bar, looking out at the amazing view. I did go for a few walks, but as it was minus ten degrees most of the time, I preferred to stay inside. I was in the casino every night until about three or four in the morning, so I was only sleeping around three hours a night. I lost a small fortune in that casino and so I was glad to be going home, where I couldn't do quite as much damage to my bank account.

It was a great trip, but I was shattered by the end of it. I slept all the way to the airport in the car and all the way home on the flight.

* * *

Another amazing trip came courtesy of my friends, Damian and Delaine Le Bas. Damian has been a good friend since school (we went to the Reading rock festivals together) and Delaine is very popular in the European art world, especially with her installations. Damian is also very talented; I have a fantastic map drawing he did framed on my bedroom wall.

Damian married Delaine (who is of gypsy heritage) thirty years ago, and I've been abroad with them both on their travels throughout Europe and Israel, helping put up Delaine's installations. One time I went with them to Graz in Austria, where I helped put up an installation, and then actually performed on the opening night of the exhibition, doing a strip for the audience. Graz is a beautiful city and everything – including my stripping – went really well.

Israel was always a place I'd wanted to visit, and so when D+D got an invitation to go to Tel Aviv, I desperately wanted to go with them. They agreed, and we went on a five day trip, staying in a nice hotel in the centre of the city.

The first day we were there, I helped put up the installation, leaving me with three days to explore and do what I wanted. It was November 2009 and the weather was great – 28 degrees in Israel compared to the 9 degrees I'd just left in England. Every morning, I would swim in the sea and relax on the stunning beach near the hotel, before setting out to see the rest of the country.

One day, I took a bus to Jerusalem. What an awe-inspiring place! I felt like I'd been there before, perhaps in a past life. I went to the Wailing Wall where I posted a prayer in one of the cracks, and everywhere I went, I had a very strong feeling like I'd been there before.

Unfortunately, a lot of Jerusalem is incredibly commercialised – almost like a Disney park – but I enjoyed my day there, and the next day, I went to Bethlehem. I had to go through passport control when I crossed the Palestinian border, and then I jumped in a taxi. The Palestinian driver was friendly, so I didn't think I'd get kidnapped or anything like that.

Anyway, I finally got to Bethlehem and visited the place where Jesus was born. It's a strange place... eerie and very quiet, but peaceful. After a couple of hours, I came back to where I'd been dropped off to find the taxi driver still there. He took me back to the border via a souvenir shop – Jonny Christmas Souvenir and café – which was obviously run by a relative of his, and I picked up a couple of crucifixes and some other bits and pieces before getting back in the taxi.

The last trip I took was an organised coach trip tour to the Dead Sea, which was pretty amazing. We went to the Sea via a load of other destinations, which I really liked, as Israel isn't that big and we got to see most of it during the drive. Finally, we got to the Dead Sea, and again I felt strange, like I had déjà vu – I felt like I'd been there before. As we approached the sea, a big thunderstorm was coming our way, apparently the first one they'd had for at least three years.

When I got in the sea itself, I lay in the warm water, floating on my back and looking up at the wild sky. It was like something out of a movie. The Dead Sea is full of salt, so I couldn't sink while floating, which is a weird yet amazing experience. After a while, I got out of the water and went into a natural hot spa to wash off all the salt, and my skin and body felt totally rejuvenated.

That evening when I got back, I watched the opening night of the exhibition – which was a big success – and the curator took us back to his house for supper before we flew home the next day.

Unfortunately, the way back didn't go quite as smoothly as the rest of the trip, as I got stopped at customs. My bag was searched and then taken away from me, and I had no idea why until they came back and explained; the Dead Sea body scrub looked like cocaine, and they had to hold me until they had a chance to check it out and see what it really was. I only just got released in time to make the flight home.

Another memorable holiday.

* * *

I've had several good – or 'interesting' experiences through Star Now, and one time it actually led to me going on a cruise around the Mediterranean.

Basically, I answered an advertisement on the site for a new dating show. It was called *Love Boat*, it was going to be held on a cruise ship, and it was going to be hosted by Brendan Sheerin, the guide from the popular channel four show, *Coach Trip*.

I was soon contacted by the production team and asked to go to their offices in North London for an interview. I was working in London at the time so I popped over and had a chat. It went well (I could feel that they liked me) and they told me that I would be the oldest contestant on the boat. After some more talking, they said they'd be in touch soon.

To be honest, I didn't think much more about it – I'd been to dozens of castings and they often don't work out – but the next week, I got a phone call from the production team, telling me that I was in. I would be flying out to Barcelona to join the MSC Splendida ship on the 14th October 2012. It was two weeks away. Woohoo!

So, on Sunday the 14th, I went up to Gatwick in the morning to meet with some of the other contestants, and after flying to Barcelona, we met up with the rest. They were a lively bunch from all over England and Scotland, and they'd started drinking in the bar at the airport. We got a coach to the harbour to see the ship, boarding that evening. The boat was beautiful, and I was given a room to share with a guy called James. He was an ex-army man, 28 from Milton Keynes, and he now worked as a prison officer – a nice bloke. To start the trip, we all went to the restaurant and had a gorgeous five course meal, followed by a few beers with James. We both wandered around the ship for a while and then turned in.

So, what exactly was *Love Boat*? Well, the idea for the show was that one guy or one girl would choose between three guys or girls to take on a date, either on the boat or on shore, at one of the ports we'd be docking at along the way.

There was a piece of paper pinned up in our rooms that told us the order of who would be choosing and who would be on the panel to be chosen. I was going to be picking between three girls on the Tuesday, so I had a whole day free to sunbathe, swim and relax before I had to do my bit. I also went to the top bar – which had panoramic views of the med and which held the set for the show – to watch the first lot of people choosing their dates. I had another perfect meal that night but didn't go to the casino with the others afterwards, instead choosing to go to bed, as I knew I'd be on TV in the morning.

So, the next day, I woke up early and went to the gym to get me in gear. Then, it was show time. I walked onto the set and sat down on the chair, looking at the three girls who were sitting on the stools in front of me.

Brendan introduced me and we chatted for a bit, and then the girls stood up individually and walked over to me, introducing themselves one at a time. They had to say why they thought they'd be a good date for me, then they had to do a little dance, and then they would go and sit back down. They were all a lot younger than me, especially Adriana, who was a tall, thin model from London.

After the girls had done their thing, I was told to go away for three hours to think about them and make my decision. After a while, I knew I'd made my mind up, although I wasn't quite sure I'd made the right choice – I could feel that the woman I'd gone for was right up herself. Still, with the decision made, I went off and chilled for a bit, having a drink with James until it was time to go back on set.

By this time the bar was full with all the other contestants and some passengers as well – about two hundred people in total. Brendan asked me to choose the girl, and I said Adriana, mainly because I knew my mates at home would like me to have a go with her.

I didn't expect what happened next.

Instead of Adriana coming over and hugging me like the contestants had done in all the other shows, she said she didn't want to go on the date, garbling on about some excuse or other.

On hearing this, Brendan quickly said, "Choose another, Rod," so I chose Gaynor, but she wasn't having any of it either, as she refused to be second best. I looked over at the last girl and she shook her head in a 'no' motion. Shit.

It was all a bit awkward, and not knowing what to do, Brendan put his arms around me and gave me a hug. The crowd didn't know what to do either, and looking over, I saw James laughing. After a few seconds of silence, Brendan said that I'd stay on the boat and be on a new panel the following day. How embarrassing!

After that, I went and had a drink or three with James and a couple of the other contestants, making sure I didn't look at those three girls during dinner. What a disaster.

The next day, however, I was over my embarrassing moment and sat on a panel of three boys for another episode. Luckily, a lady from Aberdeen – Lynsey – chose me, but not before us boys were made to go off and change into fancy dress! James and one of the girls dressed me up as a woman, with full-on makeup and a very nice wig. I could guess why Lynsey chose me. After all, she was probably nearer my age than anyone else's (she looked about forty) and she probably felt sorry for me due to the massively embarrassing moment of the day before, but I have to admit – I did look pretty damn good as a woman.

We had a lovely meal at the captain's table and were given money to spend in the casino, but I went to bed alone. I had two more splendid days on the boat before getting off at the port near Rome, from which I flew home.

At least I got a date in the end!

* * *

The experience I gained helping D+D with their installations came in handy later on, when I decided I was going to try and sell some artwork – some of Damian's art, some from the students at the art college, and a few from Dickie, my bricklayer friend who also worked for me.

Like many things in my life, it started with me mentioning it to a friend (in this case, Peter, the journalist), and ended with a quite impressive string of incidents that I never would have expected.

Basically, Peter told me that his friend was the owner of Champneys, the health club chain. He was going to be staying at the club the following weekend, and he said he would ask the owner if he would allow me to place some paintings on the wall of the club (Peter knew there were pictures on some of the corridor walls). Well, Peter came back from his weekend and immediately rang me with the news: I could display twelve paintings along a wall leading to the gym for three weeks. I never expected that! Pleased, I quickly got together twelve paintings, some classic and some very modern – a good mix, I thought. I hadn't realised Dickie could paint so well, and all of the images I chose were really good.

So, I gathered the paintings, loaded them into a van, and got driven to Champneys in Petersfield, Hampshire, by my friend Jon the plumber. Jon spent the whole day with me, placing the artwork on the walls of the corridor, which I did a pretty good job at due to my experience of arranging D+D's work. The display looked quite impressive and I priced the paintings between £300 and £1,000 each. I had no idea if any would be sold (and I didn't tell the artists what I was pricing them at) but if any did sell, I'd get a third, Champneys would get a third, and the artist would get a third.

After a few days, I got a phone call from Champneys, saying that one of the paintings had a potential buyer – the Princess of Brunei. Blimey! I went straight down there, meeting with the Princess (who was beautiful), and chatting about the artwork. I was in complete bullshit mode, but it must have worked, because she bought the painting for £800. One of her aides counted out the money right there and then, I couldn't believe it. So, the Princess went back to Brunei, taking the painting with her. A week later I sold another painting – this time, one that Dickie had done – for £450, as well as one more during those three weeks. The display also generated a lot of interest in all of the artists, so it was fruitful for everyone.

I had to laugh when I told Dickie that his painting had sold. He looked so confused, and a few seconds later, I realised why – he told me it was a painting by numbers that he'd just coloured in!

That was my first successful venture into the art selling world, and my last; while I enjoyed it, I had other ideas of what to do next, and bigger and better things to go onto.

One day, I was contacted by Alex, a photographer who'd found me through my Star Now profile page. He was gay and a fashion designer, and had done work for several celebrities, including Nigella Lawson. He wanted me to be in his online adult magazine, 'My Best Friend's Dad', and as I was interested, I went up to London to meet him in a café in Putney. He outlined what he'd like me to do, and I agreed that he could come down to my house. He was a good guy, and I could guess what he wanted photos of – after all, I had 'ex-stripper' listed on my profile page. At this time, I had some local work in East Preston, just five miles away from me, but I would be glad of the extra work with Alex.

He came down one Thursday morning and met me at Dabba's house (I'd already warned him of what I'd be doing, and he was fine with it, finding the whole thing pretty funny), where he gave me a Viagra tablet. I was glad for this – it would have been hard to raise the flag otherwise – and I went upstairs to get ready. I came back down with just an opened shirt on and a massive hard on, nothing else, and Alex got to work, taking a load of photos from all different angles while I did all sorts of poses. I had a quick look at the photographs, and they were good; I actually liked them. He said he would put them on the site as soon as he'd edited them, then he paid me £400 and signed me on with his agency. He told me he had a lot of plans and future projects, including some porn films. As an inspiring actor, I told him I'd be happy to work for him and I still am.

His site is going well, with thousands of new members joining monthly.

* * *

As a bit of an aside, at around this time I managed to locate Tabitha Ritchie again, who by then was working at a Kabbalah centre in Fulham. I emailed her and she replied, inviting me up to go out for a meal and to stay for the weekend. I had no intention of going on about the money or the work we did for her; I just liked her and wanted to get back in touch.

Once everything had been arranged, I drove up on a Friday and we met in a pub in Fulham. We immediately hit it off again, laughing and joking and remembering all the nights out we'd had whilst we were working on the project. We went for a nice Spanish meal and drank far too much, meaning I was far too gone to have sex. So, we crashed out, and the next morning we went to the borough market near London Bridge. It was amazingly busy, and we had a much needed champagne and oyster breakfast, before walking round and sampling many more drinks – cider, beer, wine, you name it.

Tabitha had arranged for us to go out that evening with two of her married friends, but by the time we got back to her flat after the market, I was exhausted and crashed out again. When she tried to wake me up to get ready for the night out, I told her I'd rather stay in. Well, she wasn't very happy about that, and we started arguing. Obviously, I must have said something that wasn't to her liking, as she told me I'd better go home. Shit. I was still so drunk and I had no idea what I'd said; I just remember wanting to get out of there. After our fight, I stormed off and stupidly drove in my car. After a while, I stopped just outside London and curled up in the back seat to sleep it off.

I've never seen or heard from Tabitha again. Oh well.

* * *

One thing I haven't mentioned in this book, but which affected me in a huge way, was the OCD I used to suffer from. This started when I was very young, when I thought I had to touch things constantly and dress in a certain way. I believed that if I did these things, I would be able to stop all the rows and the grief.

It wasn't long before I was totally controlled by this thing, and although I'm 99% better now compared to how I was, I do still have it, deep inside me. I've just learned how to control it more.

For one thing, I'd have to put my clothes on in a certain order, doing up my laces four to five times before going on to the trousers, shirts, jumpers, coats and shoes, until I'd done it in the proper way. I also had to get into bed in a certain way, open and close doors in a specific manner, all sorts of things; virtually everything I did I had to do it in some weird way. It went on and on. I'd always be the last out on the field at football, and woe betide having to do a boot up during the game!

A lot of people thought I was weird but I tried to laugh it off. Just recently, I've managed to get a hold on all my phobias, but some days they still rise up. Still, I've learnt to control them now… just…!

My OCD wasn't good when linked with religion, as for years I would bite my cheek and do other things that I viewed as forms of self-punishment; if I thought I'd done something bad or hadn't done something correctly in terms of my OCD, I would revert to this kind of behaviour.

I was brought up Catholic, and indeed, I still go to church each and every Sunday. I was confirmed (I was even an altar boy) and I try to stick by the rules as much as I can. My parents, on the other hand, didn't go to church. In fact, if my dad had stepped across the threshold, there would have been a huge thunderbolt heading his way.

The church I go to now is beautiful, with a stunning ceiling that is completely covered by an amazing painting – a reproduction of the one in the Sistine Chapel. I go every Sunday morning at 8.15 a.m. for mass. I feel peaceful there and I pray for thanks, grateful for everything I should be grateful for. I also pray for peace in this crazy world.

Well, I might not adhere to all of the catholic rules – no masturbation and no sex before marriage? No no no! To be honest, I think I'm a bit confused with all the religions. What I do believe is that I am an old soul and that I have had many past lives. I also have friends on the same level as me.

I strongly believe that in this universe – and in others – there is other life out there; we just haven't found it yet. Also, I have never understood the need to have wars over religion, and I never will.

What I think is important in this life – and what I try to do on a daily basis – is to help whenever you can, and to be nice. 'Love and light.'

* * *

Since I left the family home ten years ago, I have remained single, as I thought I would. However, I've had a few women over the years whom I'd go out and sleep with, and not all of these were the women I used to meet on websites.

One such woman was Cheryl, who I'd known since she stayed at the flat I had in Australia. We met up again a few years ago and it was good to see her. She was divorced and still living in Worthing, and we'd go out and stay in hotels on the odd occasion. She was every man's dream – still fit, with a body to die for. There was also Jo from Brighton, a spiritual healer and someone I slept with a few times. We're good friends now. Still, there's been no one that I had an actual relationship with.

I'm currently happy with my life and full of appreciation for all my friends and the people who saved my life that day at the gym.

I moved into a flat just over a year ago, and I share it with my twenty year old son, Ryan, which is great.

And the next twenty-five years? Well, I don't know what I'm going to do, but I do know that I will enjoy it, no matter what. Maybe I'll do some more writing or get a break with my acting, who knows? The fact that I have no idea is more exciting than anything else.

As I finish writing this book, my mother is in a hospice. She won't be able to read it, but I dedicate it to you, Mum xxxxx

It's been a year since the incident and I'm nearly back to my old self. Unfortunately, my fitness still isn't as good as it was twelve months ago, but I'm working on it daily and I know I'll get back to what I was before. My brain is still a bit groggy but it's getting better every day, and I'm happy to say that I can go back to driving again.

As far as work goes, I could go back to building but I don't want to do that if I can help it. Instead, I've joined up with a few more acting and modelling agencies, so I hope I can get some work in this area of employment. On that note, if there is anybody who has enjoyed reading this book and finds parts adaptable for a small film or a comedy TV programme, I would be delighted.

I've spent a lot of time on my own this past year and I've done a lot of thinking. Now I go easy on myself and I'm so much more relaxed. I'm looking forward to the rest of my life, and I have many plans to travel and explore, write, and keep fit. I still have no desire to be in a relationship; I'm happy being single. I want to thank everyone for their kindness and help over this past year.

Love and Light to you all, and if you take just one thing from this book, I hope it is this: be happy...!!!

In February I dimmed my light
For a short while
I was out of sight
The body was still
No breath to fill
A perfect peace

An early release
But no, I did return
So all of my friends
And those that prayed
My love for you
Will never fade......

Poems

All of the following poems were written by me,
Roderick Wood.

Winter's Day On Worthing Beach...

As I sit upon these stones
That dig into my bottom's bones,
I look out at this angry scene
Of walls of water, blue and green
The wind it blows a spray like sheet
Of vapour cold, a touch of sleet.
The seagulls blown across the sky
Against this wind they cannot fly
The sound so fierce of wind and sea
I watch with flask and cup of tea
My cheeks feel raw, my eyes they sting
The ocean swells, a tidal king!
No little boats out there can fish
No catch today to cook a dish,
Not many people brave this storm
All tucked away inside to warm,
To me this weather
So bleak and wild
Feels like a present to a child,
I gaze and wonder at the power
As waves explode and me do shower...
I leave the beach
The seaweed scattered
The shingle moved
The wood groynes battered
Now wonderful refreshed and new
I walk away no more to view...

Death...

So what happens when
We leave this mortal coil
Do the memories, the laughter
The moments die and spoil...
Do the thoughts and wishes
All the deeds you've done
Children that you brought up
Or maybe you had none
For me there is no end
There cannot be a cease
For what's the point of being here
A life with short term lease,
I know my soul it tells me,
Be strong and kind and pure
And learn a lot from this one
For more I will endure,
You have to love each other
And help all that you can
You have to start denying
The lust and greed that's man
Have faith in the divine you
Have faith in the unknown
Do not be scared to leave here
For guidance will be shown
I know that death is just a point
A start of something new
I know I will be learning more
And so my friend will you...

Hard Work...

The smell of smoke
A dirty joke
The air obscene
With nicotine
"I'm in, budge up!"
I gruffly shout
"Don't push, sit down
Or get back out!!"

The van is full
With all me mates,
We're off to work
The site awaits
With wellies on
And hard hat too,
Our concrete gang
A motley crew!

The trucks back in
The west slush pours,
We tamp and screed
To level these floors
We push! And pull!
And trip and fall!
"More water in this mix!"
I call!

For hours long
We sweat and toil
No time to stop
This stuff will spoil
I mop my brow
And shake my head
We grunt and groan
Our faces red

We're nearly there
The last load's out.
"Let's get this flat.
Don't muck about!"

The mixer stopped
The noise now off
We hit the caff
To munch and scoff
My back so sore
Oh what a fool
How much I wished
I stayed at school

The grease washed down
With builder's tea
Now back to work
My men and me
All tired now
Hard work, low pay
The same tomorrow
Like Groundhog Day!

But in our thoughts
A ray of light
The joy that is
A Friday night
A break and chance
For fun and laughs!
Few beers
A dance!

Forever...

My quiet thoughts
To me appear
To search myself
For why I'm here

Are my lives
To fail and win
To grow and learn
With death begin

I ask my soul
To be so clear
To love what is
And have no fear...

Autumn Walk...

The yellow brown and golden sound,
There gently gliding to the ground

No wind today to speed their fall,
The leaves float down from trees so tall

The dew drops on the grass so clear,
A fresh chilled air as winter's near

A mist wrapped round a distant wood,
A cloak of white with ghostly hood

The land it lends itself to sleep
For future nights so long and deep

The sunlight of the dusk it fades
A cloak of darkened cloud invades

So autumn's here and with it brings
The bedtime yawn of nature's things...

The Wind

It grumbles, bangs and throws its voice,
It smashes, tears, it has no choice,
It pushes up the clouds of dust,
It drives the rainfall in a thrust!
It bends the trees
It whips the seas
It brings all nature to its knees
It can blow hot
It can blow cold
It has no mercy, to new or old
But when it's calm
And all at ease
It can bring comfort in a breeze...

Lightning Source UK Ltd.
Milton Keynes UK
UKOW07f1127020415

248917UK00010B/18/P